step-by-step *head*

massage

step-by-step *head*
massage

Eilean Bentley

Gaia Books Limited

A Gaia original

Books from Gaia celebrate the vision of Gaia, the self-sustaining living Earth, and seek to help its readers live in greater personal and planetary harmony.

Editors	Katherine Pate, Sarah Townsend
Designer	Mark Epton
Art Director	Lucy Guenot
Photographer	Steve Teague
Managing Editor	Pip Morgan
Production	Lyn Kirby
Direction	Joss Pearson, Patrick Nugent

GAIA ®

First published in the United Kingdom in 2000 by Gaia Books Ltd, 66 Charlotte Street, London W1P 1LR and 20 High Street, Stroud, Gloucestershire GL5 1AZ

ISBN 1-85675-101-5

A catalogue record of this book is available from the British Library

Printed and bound in Singapore by Kyodo

10 9 8 7 6 5 4 3 2 1

Note on safety
The techniques and treatments in this book are to be used at the reader's sole discretion and risk. Always observe the cautions and consult a doctor if you are in any doubt about a medical condition.

The worldwide availability of this book in the English language has made it necessary to adopt US spellings in certain circumstances, for example, center, color.

About this book

This step-by-step guide shows you how to use a unique combination of head massage, and meditations or visualizations, to promote health and wellbeing in mind, body, and spirit.

The introduction explains how the massage and meditation techniques combine to form a truly holistic therapy, working with the body's life force, or energy.

Chapter one presents the basic techniques, while chapter two explains how to use meditation and visualization. These are then combined in a self-care routine in chapter three.

Chapter four focuses on using meditation to develop the senses, and chapter five presents the complete massage plan.

Regular head massage following the routines in chapters three and five has many health benefits. In addition, chapter six gives techniques to treat 25 common ailments and conditions.

Cautions

Head massage is very safe, but some people should be treated with care. Cautions relating to specific steps of the massage are explained in the step-by-step treatments. Please also observe the following.

The very young, the elderly, and those suffering from bone problems
Use light massage only. Pressure should not exceed the weight of your fingers: even the weight of your hand can be excessive.

Sufferers of epilepsy and clinical depression
The top of the head is a particularly sensitive area for these conditions. Use light massage only, no more than stroking and combing with your fingers.

Pregnant women
Head massage can be of great benefit during pregnancy but some special care is needed. Follow the guidelines given on page 127 in chapter six.

Cancer sufferers
Those being treated for any form of cancer, and those in remission, need extra care. A light head massage treatment will be of great benefit, but as the lymphatic system can transfer some forms of cancer to other parts of the body, avoid working on the lymphatic areas illustrated on page 107.

Sufferers of low blood pressure
Head massage lowers the blood pressure, so anyone who already has low blood pressure should have only a light treatment lasting no longer than 15 minutes.

Contents

Introduction

Introduction

Good health depends on balanced energy. This energy, called chi or ki in Oriental medicine, or prana in Indian tradition, is the life force itself. It permeates our bodies and every living thing in the universe. When our energy is unbalanced we may feel mildly irritable, out of sorts, or even seriously unwell.

Stress, poor diet, strong emotions, or toxin build-up are all symptoms of modern living that can unbalance life energy and create areas of negativity. The power of energy healing lies in rebalancing the life force so that the flow of energy within us is constant, effortless, and unblocked. Head massage, combined with simple meditative techniques, provides a simple and effective way to rebalance our energies and clear any areas of negativity, easing and even preventing many illnesses.

Many of the head massage techniques in this book are based on traditional Indian head massage. Some are drawn from other ancient and traditional methods of healing such as shiatsu, reiki, acupressure, and qi gong. Although each uses different terminology to explain the theory, they are all based on a common concept. Life energy flows within us and, by working on the channels it flows through, or specific points or areas, this energy can be brought into balance.

Head massage also affects the pulsing rhythms of cerebrospinal fluid, carrying healing messages around the body and stimulating the body's self-healing mechanisms. Tension in the muscles is released, dispersing toxins, reducing mental and physical stress, and improving blood flow to the brain.

Sharing head massage

You can use any head massage strokes on yourself, and a self-care routine is introduced in chapter three. However, the treatment is much more effective if someone else massages you, as they can talk you through the meditations or visualizations, while you relax and let go completely. Sharing the experience with a friend or partner, and taking turns to give a massage, greatly enhances the healing qualities of the techniques. You will both benefit as much from the giving as the receiving.

Touch alone is very powerful, but another vital ingredient in head massage is the intention of the giver to transmit healing, caring, love, and wellbeing to the receiver. The meditations and visualizations that accompany the massage techniques help here: by centering and grounding the giver, and channeling the feelings and emotions, they allow the receiver to take an active part in their own healing.

Meditations and visualizations allow you to tap into the universal healing energy and transmit this to your partner. By calming the mind, meditation allows this energy to flow freely. Visualization enables you to direct it to specific areas where it is needed, either within your body or in your aura – the energy field surrounding your physical body. Many illnesses originate in energy disturbances in the aura, so using visualization to cleanse it is an effective preventive treatment. The combination of massage and meditation is a truly holistic therapy that benefits the entire mental, emotional, spiritual, and physical being.

This book is not just about giving and receiving a relaxing massage. It is about the energies of two people becoming completely as one, for the benefit of the healing process.

Positions for treatment

Traditional Indian head massage is usually given with the receiver seated. However, some people prefer to be massaged lying down. You should choose whichever feels more comfortable for you and your partner.

With your partner sitting it is very easy to reach all areas of the head, neck, and shoulders. However this position may not be ideal for really deep massage. The more relaxed your partner becomes, the more she will slump in the chair, which can become rather uncomfortable for both of you. Only light, simple meditations can be used, such as asking your partner to focus on rippling waves or color changes in a crystal.

For a deep, relaxing massage it may be better for your partner to lie on her back on the floor, on some padding such as an exercise mat, or a couple of duvets. In this position the body can enter a state of deep relaxation, allowing its own healing mechanisms to work. Now you can use a strong meditation or visualization as part of the treatment, such as floating down a river or flying through clouds, to help with the healing process.

However, it is more difficult to reach areas on the back of the head and neck with your partner lying down, and you will often have to turn the head to the side and support it with your hand. You will need to kneel or sit behind your partner's head, and may have to move around to reach different areas.

Whichever position your partner chooses, you need to be relaxed and comfortable yourself in order to guide her into deep relaxation. Wear loose fitting clothing so you can move around easily, especially if you are working on the floor. If you need to change position during the treatment, move slowly and rhythmically so your partner is unaware of any break.

To work with your partner seated, select a chair that is high enough for you to reach the scalp and shoulders without bending. Your partner should sit with feet flat on the floor, hands in her lap, and shoulders back. Stand squarely behind her. You should wear comfortable shoes or have bare feet, and maintain a straight posture.

Creating a soothing atmosphere

Before starting a treatment you should prepare yourself and your surroundings. The room should be comfortably warm, but not stuffy. Lower the lighting or use candles, and burn incense or oil. It is a good idea to check first if your partner has any preferences, as smells have very different associations for different individuals. Some suggestions are given in the box below. Some people like to play soothing music, others prefer silence. Choose whatever feels best for you and your partner.

If it is not possible to burn oils or play music, perhaps at the office, you can still prepare the space by clearing away any clutter and making sure you will not be interrupted while you are massaging your partner.

Essential oils

Lavender	lifts the spirits
Sandalwood	relieves stress and lifts the spirits
White pine	creates a feeling of space and openness
Geranium	lifts the mood
Eucalyptus	treats the first symptoms of cold and respiratory problems
Frankincense	relaxes, uplifts, relieves depression, and creates a feeling of sacred space
Citrus	clears the head and lifts the spirits

Cleansing visualizations

Before you begin to massage your partner, you can perform this simple visualization to cleanse the energy of the space in which you are working.

Sit for a few moments in the middle of the space. Close your eyes and visualize a gold ring spinning just above your head. Watch it growing larger and descending so that it comes down around your body, leaving behind a golden trace as it descends, enveloping you in a bubble. Watch the energy within this bubble turn to a soft pink, and move this energy outward from you until it fills the whole space or room.

You have now surrounded yourself in a protective energy field, which will stop any negative energy from your partner reaching you, and vice versa. You have created a healing space filled with this protective energy.

At the end of your massage session, after you have broken contact with your partner, use this visualization to clear your energy and the energy of the space.

Sit for a few moments and again visualize the space filled with pink, healing energy. Slowly bring the bubble in around you. See the gold ring spinning beneath you. Move the ring up around your body until it is above your head. Feel the energy rising up through your body with the gold ring. Then watch the ring grow smaller and slowly rise up out of sight.

Making and breaking the energy connection

Before any massage session with a partner you should make an energy connection between you. This enables you to tap into the healing energy of the universe and allow it to channel through you into your partner, maximizing the healing power of the treatment. It also synchronizes you both, allowing you to understand your partner's needs instinctively.

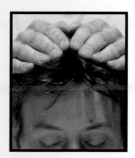

At the end of a treatment it is equally important to break the connection between you. This allows you both to take back complete control of your own energy flow, as well as sending any negative energy back into the universe to be cleansed. No links will remain that could drain your energy or your partner's. This may seem a strange concept, but the more sensitive you become to the flowing of energy, the more you will appreciate its movements, directions, and strengths.

Full instructions for making and breaking the energy connection are given in the massage plans.

After a treatment, you should allow time for your partner to come back to reality. A deeply relaxing massage can leave the recipient feeling a little light-headed. Spend some time chatting quietly and have a cup of tea or other non-alcoholic drink until you both feel more grounded.

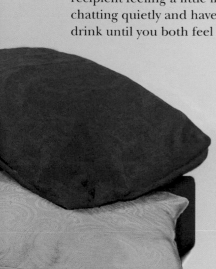

chapter one
Basic techniques

This chapter presents the basic techniques used in head, neck, and shoulder massage. Follow the step-by-step instructions, working on yourself or on a partner, to familiarize yourself with the techniques and to start to feel their power.

Basic techniques

The position of points and areas to massage are often described using fingerwidths; for example, "massage along the jawbone at two fingerwidth intervals". Because parts of the body are in proportion, and someone with small hands will usually also have a small overall bone structure, using your massage partner's personal fingerwidth measurement helps you locate the correct areas on that person. So before you start to give a massage, look at the width of your partner's index finger and use that measurement when necessary.

Always use both hands in massage. If you are working with one hand only, use the other to support your partner. This maintains and strengthens the contact between you, and helps to relax your partner and hold him in position.

For all the techniques in this chapter – unless specified otherwise – sit your partner in a chair and stand squarely behind him. Most of the movements described require you to work in regular lines over the head and upper body (see illustration opposite). This is reassuring for your partner, as he then knows where to expect the next touch. It also helps to ensure that you cover the whole area effectively.

When you have finished using one technique, stroke or gently comb through your partner's hair with your fingers. This relaxing and soothing action loosens the hair ready for the next treatment. If you have been supporting your partner's head with your hand, it also allows him to take control of his head again before you move to a new position.

Let your partner guide you on how much pressure to use. Too light a pressure can be irritating, but the massage should not cause discomfort.

Caution

Do not use firm pressure on the top of the head on the very young, the elderly, or anyone suffering from epilepsy, bone disease, or clinical depression. Also observe the cautions on page 5.

Rotations

This technique should be used in a slow, meditative way. You can use one or more fingers, your thumbs, the heel of your hand, or your whole hand. Work in regular lines over your partner (see below, right) to help him relax and enjoy the experience.

These movements stimulate the circulation, move stagnant blood and energy, and tone and loosen the muscles. Rotations on the head also stimulate the scalp and improve hair condition.

One finger rotations
Cup your right hand on the forehead, taking care not to push down on the eyebrows. Place the pad of the index or middle finger of your left hand in the centre of the forehead at the hairline. Using firm pressure, rotate your finger for three to five seconds. Then move two fingerwidths back along the midline and repeat the rotation. Continue until you reach the nape of the neck.

Working in lines
Now place your finger on the hairline two fingerwidths to the left of your first line. Work back in a line parallel to the first, ending at the nape of the neck. Continue to work lines back over the head until you have covered the left half, finishing with a line running just above the ear. Stroke the hair gently with both hands, then use your right hand to work back in lines on the right side of the head.

Rotations

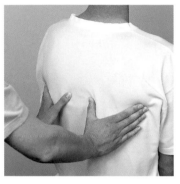

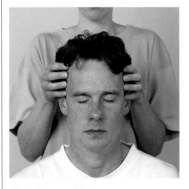

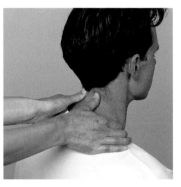

Rotations with two or more fingers

Using two or more fingers reduces the amount of pressure you exert, while allowing you to cover a greater area. Start with your fingers about 1cm (½in) apart on the hairline, and work back over the head in lines as for one finger rotations.

If you start in the middle of the hairline with all four fingers you will be able to cover the top of the head down to the nape of the neck in one sweep. You can then use the four fingers of both hands, one either side of the head, to work both sides of the head together.

Thumb rotations: back

This technique is used on the upper back, shoulders, and neck, but not on the head as it exerts strong pressure. To increase the pressure further, lean into your thumbs as you work.

Place the pads of your thumbs either side of the spine, level with the base of the shoulder blades and rotate firmly for three to five seconds. Then move your thumbs two fingerwidths outward in a horizontal line and rotate again. Repeat, moving two fingerwidths along this line each time, until you reach the edges of the back.

Now start either side of the spine again, two fingerwidths up from your first line, and work a parallel line. Repeat until you reach the neck.

Caution
Do not apply strong pressure directly on the spine.

Thumb rotations: neck

Rest your fingers on the shoulders and use thumb rotations in horizontal lines from each side of the spine outward until you reach the base of the skull.

Caution
Do not massage this part of the neck on anyone who has cancer.

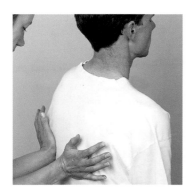

Heel of hand rotations: back

This technique uses firm pressure over a larger area than the thumb rotations. To increase the pressure, lean into your hands as you work. Start with the heels of your hands on either side of the spine, level with the lower edge of the shoulder blades. Rotate, using strong pressure and small movements. Then move two fingerwidths outward on a horizontal line and repeat. Continue out to the edges and then in parallel lines up the back, as for thumb rotations.

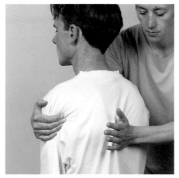

Increasing the pressure

For stronger pressure, brace your partner with your arm across the front of the shoulders and use one hand to work parallel lines over one half of the back. Change hands and repeat on the other side.

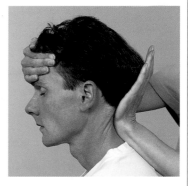

Heel of hand rotations: head

Support the forehead carefully with one hand, place the heel of your hand at the nape of the neck and rotate using small, gentle movements. Work a line up the middle of the head and over the top to the forehead.
This movement can also be used on the sides of the head, working in lines from the back of the head to the front (see rotations with two or more fingers, page 20).

Whole hand rotations

To apply a lighter pressure over a larger area, use the whole hand, following the movements for heel of hand rotations.

Pressure

For this technique you can use your fingers, thumbs, hands, or elbows, and lean in with your body weight to vary the amount of pressure used. When working on very tense areas of your partner's body, a continuous whole-body rocking action of pressure and release is very effective. Alternatively, keep the massage quiet and still, holding the pressure for three to five seconds before moving to the next point.

This technique loosens tension and stiffness in muscles and is particularly effective in treating stress and tension headaches. It also balances and boosts energy levels, and subtly corrects pressure imbalances in the cerebrospinal fluid.

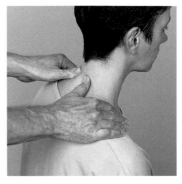

Thumb pressure
Use thumbs together or separately to apply pressure to the upper back, shoulders, and neck. Before exerting strong pressure, ask your partner to brace herself by pressing her hands against her knees.
Start with your thumbs either side of the spine, level with the bottom of the shoulder blades. Lean forward, with your weight on your thumbs, hold for three to five seconds, then release. Work outward from the spine in parallel horizontal lines up the back. At the base of the neck, use your thumbs on either side of the spine. Press upward for three to five seconds, release, and move two fingerwidths to the next point. Continue until you reach the nape of the neck. Alternatively, work with one thumb, supporting your partner with your other arm across the front of the shoulders. Work across one half of the back from the spine outward and give the back a vigorous rub before changing hands and working on the other side.

Caution
Do not massage this part of the neck on anyone who has cancer.

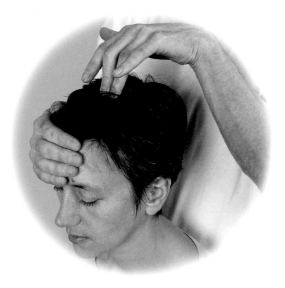

Finger pressure
Support the head with your left hand. Starting in the middle of the hairline, use one or more fingers to apply a firm pressure for three to five seconds, then release. Cover one half of the head, working back in parallel lines to the nape of the neck, then change hands and work over the other half.

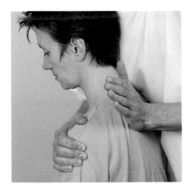

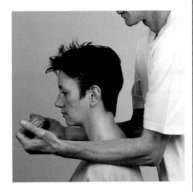

Heel of hand pressure

This technique applies less intense pressure over a larger area, and is more comfortable for very tender areas. You can use it on the back, neck, shoulders, and back of the head. Support your partner with one arm across the front of her shoulders and lean your weight slowly onto the heel of the other hand. Gently increase the pressure outward from the spine, across the back as before and moving up in lines until you reach the neck. Change hands and work on the other half of the back, then give the whole area a vigorously rub.

To use this technique on the back of the head, support your partner's forehead with one hand.

Elbow pressure

Strong pressure from the elbows is good for releasing tension in the shoulders. Standing behind your partner, place your elbows on the tops of her shoulders, close to the base of the neck. Then raise your hands back toward you, leaning your body weight onto the shoulders. Hold for three to five seconds, then release the pressure, dropping your hands forward again. Repeat at four fingerwidth intervals along the shoulders until you reach the tops of the arms.

Caution

Do not massage the midpoint of the shoulders of anyone who is pregnant.

Forearm pressure

This technique can be used to release tension in the shoulders if the area is tender. With your hands held in loose fists, rest the backs of your forearms on the tops of the shoulders, close to the base of the neck. Lean down firmly and hold for three to five seconds, then rock your body back to release. Repeat at four fingerwidth intervals along the tops of the shoulders.

Rolling

This technique is used on the head, neck, and shoulders. Use the outside edge of the hands, rolling along the line of the little fingers with a constant flowing rhythm.

Rolling relaxes mind and body, tones the scalp, and helps to ease tension.

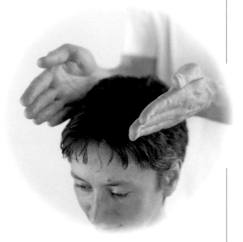

Using both hands together enables you to work on both sides of the head simultaneously. With your fingers straight, use the outside edge of the heels of your hands to make contact with the sides of the head. Now roll the pressure up the edges of your hands to the tips of your little fingers. Roll back down to the heels of the hands, maintaining a smooth rhythm. Move two fingerwidths up the head each time, following parallel lines, to cover the whole area.
For a stronger treatment, roll with one hand at a time, supporting the head with the other.

Knuckling

This technique uses the knuckles on the head, neck, and shoulders. For less pressure you can use the top set of knuckles, just below the fingernails.

This is a vigorous and stimulating treatment, which boosts energy levels and encourages deeper breathing.

Curl your hands into fists and rest them on the shoulders. Rock the fists from side to side, from the little finger to the index finger and back again. The pressure should be firm and steady. Move slowly all over the head and shoulders, following parallel lines. On the neck, start next to the spine and work outward in parallel lines moving up to the nape.

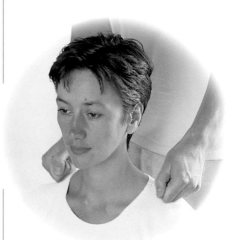

Caution
Do not massage the midpoint of the shoulders of anyone who is pregnant.

Pulling

In these techniques the hair is pulled slowly and evenly, without tweaking, to stimulate the muscles under the scalp.

Pulling releases tension in these muscles and can be used to treat tension headaches. It also conditions the hair by stimulating blood flow to the scalp.

Lying down
Start at the front of the head. Turn your hands so the palms face outward, and push your fingers through the hair from the temples. Grip the hair firmly between your fingers and pull steadily and firmly.

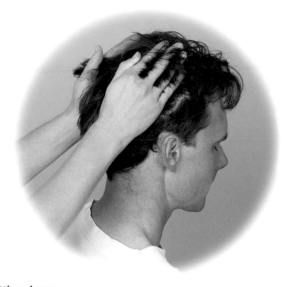

Sitting down
Start by combing your fingers lightly through the hair to loosen it. With your hands on either side of the neck, slide them up into the hair, fingers apart, keeping close to the scalp. When you have gathered a handful of hair, close your fingers firmly and pull away from the head. Allow the hair to move through your fingers under tension, creating a strong, even pull. Repeat all over the head, always pulling the hair at right angles away from the scalp.

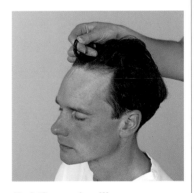

Twisting and pulling
Starting in the middle of the hairline, wrap a small section of hair around your finger and hold firmly for three to five seconds. Release and repeat two fingerwidths back along the midline to the nape of the neck. Return to the hairline and work in parallel lines to cover each side of the head in turn. Run your fingers up through the hair from the nape of the neck to the front of the head, to ease out the scalp.

Kneading

Use finger or thumb kneading on the head or face, or knead with the heel of your hand or lightly clenched fist on the head, neck, back, and shoulders.

Kneading is a wonderfully stimulating and energizing massage technique.

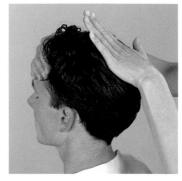

Heel of hand kneading
Support the forehead carefully with one hand. Place the heel of the other hand at the nape of the neck, applying pressure while rolling from the heel up over the palm to the fingertips. Work up to the front of the head along the midline. Then work up the sides in the same way, starting at the nape each time.

Finger kneading
Support the head with your left hand. Using the middle finger of your right hand to press on your right index finger, start in the middle of the hairline and work back along the midline at two fingerwidth intervals. Knead in parallel lines over the sides of the head. For stronger pressure, use the thumb for kneading.

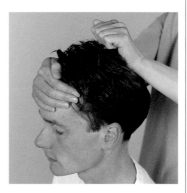

Clenched fist kneading
Clench your hand loosely into a fist, and press as you roll up from the heel of your hand to the knuckles. Work up the head in the same way as for heel of hand kneading.

Scratching

For this technique, used on the head, nails need to be short to avoid snagging your partner's scalp.

Scratching stimulates blood flow to the scalp, improving the flow of nutrients to the hair roots.

Hold your hands with your fingers together and bent so that your nails are in line. This reduces the strength you can exert and lessens the chance of catching your partner's scalp. Scratch all over the scalp with swift, light movements, keeping your wrists flexible so your nails move loosely from side to side. Make sure that you cover the whole of the head.

Pulsing

For this technique your partner should lie on her back. The weight of the body increases the pressure on the back and neck.

Pulsing eases tired muscles, loosens stiffness in the neck, back, and shoulders, and relaxes the mind and body.

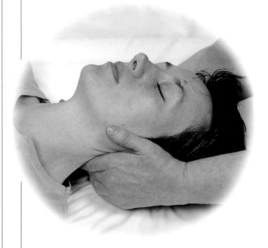

Kneel on the floor at the top of your partner's head. Slide your hands, palms upward, down under the back as far as you can reach. Now make a claw shape with your hands, with fingertips level. Move your hands alternately in small steps, up the back and toward you, so your fingertips apply moving pressure up into the back. When you reach the neck turn your hands so that the neck rests across your index fingers. Moving your hands alternately, lift the neck and pull up and back toward you, smoothly and rhythmically with firm pressure. Repeat for three or four minutes, until you feel the neck relax.

Tapping

This is a light technique that can be used on all areas.

Tapping with one or two fingers can be gentle and soothing, while tapping with all the fingers is very vigorous and stimulating.

Hold your hands so your fingertips are level. Keeping your wrists loose, and with both hands tapping together, bounce your fingertips off the hair with quick, light, smooth movements. Move over the head in regular lines, keeping a regular rhythm.

Hacking

This technique can be used on all areas, but be careful to use only gentle pressure on the top of the head.

Hacking on the back, neck, and shoulders loosens the muscles and encourages deep breathing, while hacking on the head invigorates and stimulates the mind.

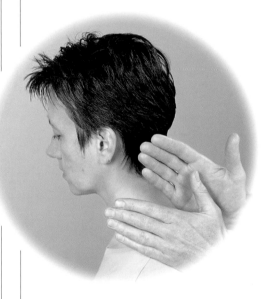

Beat with the side of each hand alternately in a light chopping action all over the head, neck, back, and shoulders, keeping a regular rhythm.

Scalp pinching

This technique can be used instead of hair pulling if your partner has very short hair or is balding.

It has the same effect of loosening and releasing tension in the scalp, to relieve tension headaches and to allow the free flow of nutrients to the scalp surface.

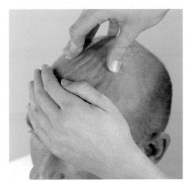

Step two
Now place your hand on the top of the head across the midline and pinch the scalp between your thumb and fingers. Hold for three to five seconds. Move back two fingerwidths and repeat. Continue in this way down to the nape of the neck.

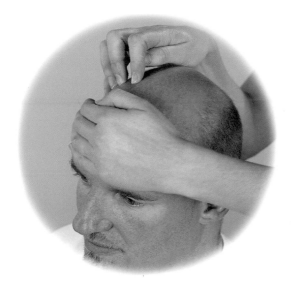

Step one
Support the forehead with one hand and place the fingers of your other hand along the hairline at the top of the forehead, just to the side of the midline. Press firmly for three to five seconds. Then with your fingers in the same position, rotate firmly for a count of five. This pressure and rotation loosens the scalp for the pinching. Repeat all over the head in lines, over the top and sides of the head.

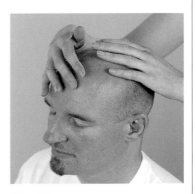

Step three
Next, work a line across one side of the head. Stroke over the head for a few moments as you change hands, and then repeat on the other side.

chapter two
Meditation and visualization

Meditation and visualization can help you to relax deeply, allowing your body's own self-healing processes to work. This chapter shows you how to combine these techniques with head massage for effective healing.

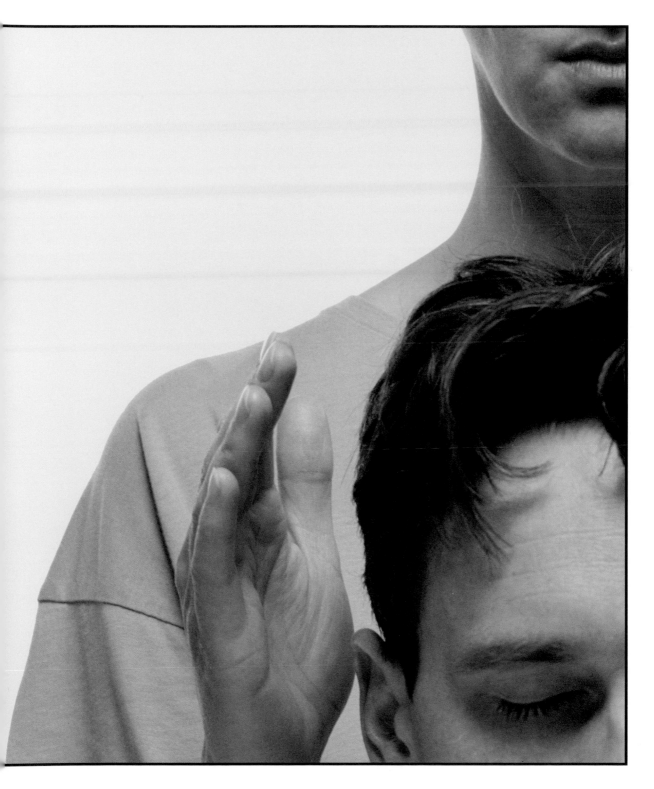

Meditation and visualization

Using meditation and visualization with head massage helps you achieve a depth of awareness, stillness, and relaxation that you cannot reach through the physical techniques alone. Together they bring about a completeness in which you and your partner share a unique sense of oneness. This, in turn, greatly amplifies the strength and effectiveness of the treatment.

The dictionary defines meditation as "deep reflection" and visualization as "forming a mental image of something not visible". The difference between the techniques becomes clear if you look at the way both are used in therapy.

During a meditation you focus on an image. This may have color, texture, shape, scent, and some small movement, for example, the candle in the meditation on page 34 in this chapter. Deep concentration and effort are required to achieve a state of relaxed stillness and oneness. In head massage, meditations are used to enhance relaxation, during which the whole of your body is treated to a healing session.

In a visualization your mind travels a journey and your imagination takes you into another reality. From there the visualization seems to take on a life of its own, and your mind and body are carried with it. In the cloud visualization on page 36 your mind is directed to harness the powerful energies of the earth, sky, sun, and water to balance the energies of your body. You can simply allow the healing processes to flow, or you can focus and direct healing to any part of your body, mind, or spirit.

Creative journeying

Visualization has its roots in ancient shamanic traditions, which form a part of many belief systems and ritual practices. True shamans would communicate with animals, plants, rocks, the earth and sky, and other beings, to gain knowledge to help their people. Nowadays hypnotherapy, psychotherapy, and brainstorming sessions all originate from shamanic tradition.

Through visualization you can connect with your subconscious mind, to solve problems, gain different perspectives, or improve your health.

Using the techniques

You can use the meditation and visualization in this chapter as you work through the self care routine in chapter three, or the complete massage plan in chapter five. These chapters also include other meditations and visualizations: choose whichever appeals to you at the time. For the self-care routine you may find it easier to record the words of the meditation or visualization first and play them as you massage, so your mind can be guided as you work with your hands.

While massaging a partner, talk through the meditation as you work slowly and rhythmically, always maintaining physical and mental contact. Your words and actions should blend seamlessly to create an almost trance-like state in which you are both in tune with the images of the meditation.

First, make sure your surroundings are warm, comfortable, free from distractions, quiet, and peaceful. Lower the lighting, burn incense or oil, play rhythmic, soft music, and allow the rest of the world to go its own way without involving you.

Spend a few moments in silence before starting, to enable you both to connect with the energies of your surroundings. Allow a feeling of ease and comfort to envelop you.

The following breathing exercise prepares you and your partner for the meditation or visualization.

Take a few slow breaths. First, inhale and exhale for a count of three. Then use a count of four. Continue increasing the count by one for each inhalation and exhalation until you reach ten. Then take three more breaths to a count of ten, filling your lungs completely. Now take a long breath and hold it for a count of five before letting it go in a short, sharp burst.

Now forget your breathing; forget everything; just be aware.

Take your awareness to the top of your head, as if you are seeing it as a detached observer. Slowly move it down your body, feeling a wave of warmth flowing down your body as you do so. As the warmth flows through you, you begin to feel more and more relaxed, heavy, and away from the rest of the world.

Now start the meditation or visualization. If your mind drifts to everyday problems, don't fight it. Allow these thoughts to pass through and simply observe them. Slowly they will drift away.

Candle meditation

Imagine a small lighted candle, deep inside your abdomen.

Breathe in, and exhale into the candle flame. The flame grows bigger.

Breathe in and exhale into the flame again. Again it grows. Keep breathing in this way until you can see and feel the candle filling your whole body.

With the next in-breath and exhalation the flame expands beyond your body, extending to about one metre (three feet) outside you.

Now be aware of the warm, golden flame all around you. Don't try to think about it, just feel it.

Observe the flame, noticing that it slowly changes color. You can control this by inhaling and exhaling into the flame.

Stay with each color, breathing gently until you feel at one with it. Feel the healing qualities of each color as it passes over you. Then slowly move to the next.

Breathe in and exhale and the color changes from gold to deep yellow.

When you are ready to move on, take a deep breath and change the color to a soft green. Relax into it.

With the next deep breath and exhalation the color becomes turquoise.

Breathe again and the color deepens to blue.

Now gently change the color to mauve. As you observe the flame this deepens to purple.

Take a breath and the color changes to a crystal clear pink, then slowly deepens to red, and then orange.

With the next breath the orange slowly lightens to yellow and the flame returns to its warm golden glow.

Stay with this golden light until you feel ready to return to everyday consciousness.

When you are ready, allow the flame to grow smaller. With each breath you take, exhale into the flame and see it growing smaller, until it is a tiny light within your abdomen again, containing all the energy and healing power of the colors and light you have seen.

Allow yourself to return slowly to the room and full awareness, feeling refreshed, energized, and wonderfully alive.

Cloud visualization

Imagine you are in the middle of a wood on a warm summer's day. The light is dappled, the shade of the trees is cool and comfortable. Take a while to make this scene as real as you can. See, smell, and feel the different trees, shrubs, flowers, and grasses, the earthiness of the woodland.

Feel your body blending with the character of the surrounding landscape.

Now visualize yourself standing on the bank of a small lake in the heart of the wood. You can see the trees and other plants all around the lake. You can feel the soft muddy ground beneath your feet. You can smell the damp earthiness.

As you look out across the lake you see a mist rising slowly from its surface.

This mist moves toward you and gradually surrounds you. As it swirls around you it feels comfortable, supportive, gentle as the summer breeze. Allow yourself to be supported by the mist. Feel yourself becoming a part of it.

Your body feels lighter and lighter. You are aware that you are growing larger as you become part of the mist. You and the mist are together as one. There is no separation between you and the mist.

You are becoming a loose collection of molecules, drifting higher and higher into the air. You can see the earth far below as you rise higher and higher.

You are spreading out and becoming a soft, light cloud. Feel the tiny atoms of your body that is the cloud. Enjoy this weightlessness and freedom. Feel the energy of the sky, the sun, and the earth below.

Now look down to the earth. You can see the wood and the lake, and a figure standing by the lake. That figure is you.

You are aware that your body is becoming heavier as the cloud condenses to make rain.

You can see tiny rainbows in your body as the raindrops form and the sunlight shines through them.

Gently, you start to fall as rain down on to the wood and the lake.

As you reach the water you can feel yourself forming into a mist floating on the surface.

Lightly, slowly, you float across the water to the figure on the shore.

You feel yourself returning into your body, standing by the shore.

When you are ready, take a few deep breaths and bring yourself back to reality. You will feel energized, refreshed, renewed, and full of light as you come back to the room and become aware of your surroundings.

chapter three
Self-care routine

This self-massage plan shows how to work on your head, back, neck, and shoulders to stimulate the energy throughout your whole body. Use this 20-minute routine daily to invigorate your system.

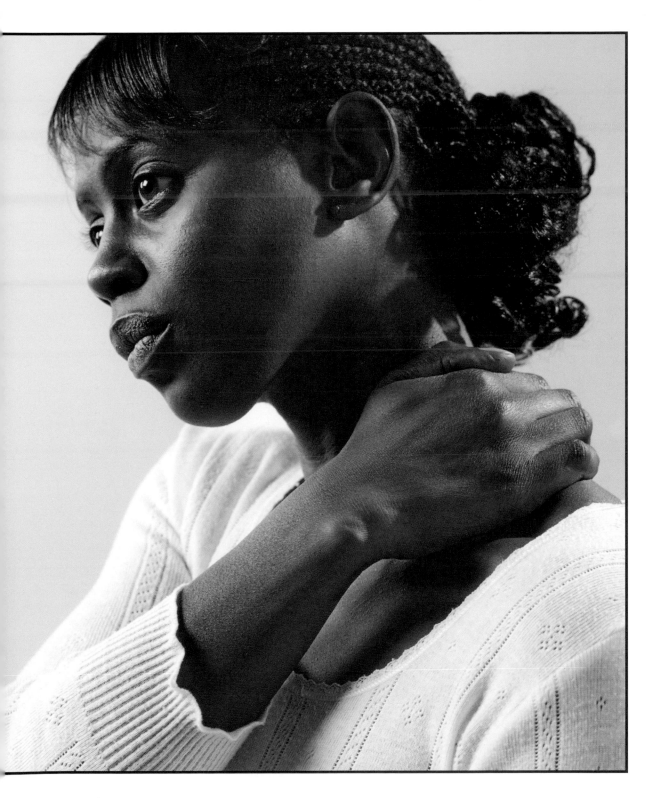

Self-care routine

Before starting the self-care routine, take time to prepare your surroundings: soften the lighting, play soothing music, and burn essential oils (see page 13). Taking time to do this enables you to relax and distance yourself from the rest of the world, thus allowing self-healing to take place.

Now prepare yourself. After centering yourself (see below), follow the golden light meditation on page 41, or use the cleansing visualization on page 14 to create a healing space and reach a place of stillness where you can work effectively.

Once you are familiar with the steps of the routine you may wish to use a simple meditation, such as the water meditation on page 100, as you massage yourself. It may help to record the words of the meditation first so that you don't have to think about it, you can just be.

When you have completed all the steps in the routine, finish with the gold ring visualization on page 56, or the candle meditation on page 34.

Centering yourself

Allow your breathing to become slow and gentle and then spend a few moments observing it, without trying to control it. Consciously become aware of every part of your body. Starting at your head and moving down, look at each part in turn as if you were a detached observer. Notice any tightness and let it go. Take as long as you need for this process.

Caution
Observe the cautions on page 5.

Golden light meditation

Forget time, it no longer exists. The world outside no longer exists.

Imagine that you are floating in the night sky. You are warm and comfortable, weightless and without any particular form. You are aware of your body but it no longer has any constricting boundaries.

Now you can feel a golden light coming toward you from far away in the universe. This is the universal healing energy, coming to renew and regenerate you.

The light enters the top of your head. It fills your head. Feel the power of the light, feel its warmth, color, and vibration.

Allow the light to move down to your neck and shoulders. It relaxes your neck and shoulders. You can feel a warmth moving down your body with the light.

Let the light move down your arms. Feel its strengthening power.

Now the light moves down through your chest and into your abdomen. It fills your body. Warmth and power follow, energizing and healing.

The light moves down your legs and out through the soles of your feet. Feel its surging power.

You are part of a vast golden wheel of light. The light comes down from the universe, through your body, out of your feet, and back up to the universe in a continuous circle.

As the light comes from the universe it brings positive energy into your body. As it returns to the universe it takes with it any negative energy. Stay with this circle for a while. Feel it strengthening and healing.

When you are ready, allow the light to fade gently. Slowly bring yourself back to the room, ready to commence your head massage.

Try to hold on to the stillness of this meditation while you work.

Neck sequence

This massage sequence for the neck will help to keep you supple well into old age. You should only use this technique for self-treatment, as it is easy to overdo it while working on someone else.

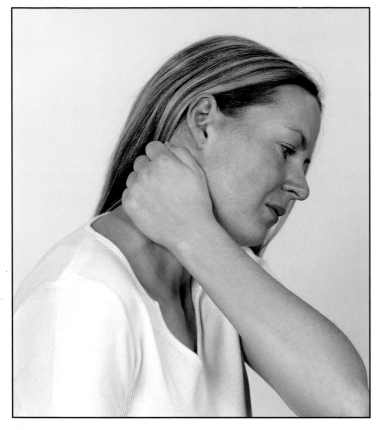

Caution
If you have a history of neck problems, you should consult your doctor before using this sequence.

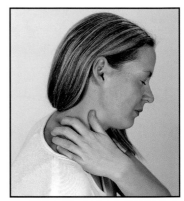

Step two
Starting again at the base of your skull, knead with your fingers down the opposite side of your neck and across your shoulders, along the same line as in Step one. Press as hard as you can. Then change hands and repeat on the other side.

Step one
Clench the fist of one hand and beat with your knuckles on the opposite side of your neck. Work a line down from the base of your skull to the outside edge of your shoulder. Do this as hard as you can bear, two or three times, then change hands and repeat on the other side.

Step three

Hold the top right side of your head with your left hand, and place the heel of your right hand on the left side of your chin. Pulling with your left hand and pushing with your right, gently twist your head round to the right as far as you can. Hold this position for a count of 30, then slowly release and bring your head back upright. Change hands and repeat on the other side, this time turning to the left.

Step four

Again, hold the top right side of your head with your left hand, and place the heel of your right hand on the left side of your chin. This time, push with your right hand and pull with your left, gently tilting your head over to the left, with your ear moving toward your shoulder. Hold for a count of 30, then release slowly and bring your head back upright. Change hands and repeat, this time tilting your head to the right. If you cannot maintain the hold for a count of 30, start with a count of 10 and slowly build up to 30.

Head sequence

Self-massage on the head is invigorating and stimulating. By loosening the muscles of the scalp it helps to prevent tension headaches and also allows blood to flow to the hair roots more easily, improving hair condition. Head massage also affects the pulsing rhythm of the cerebrospinal fluid, allowing it to carry healing messages to other parts of the body.

Caution
Do not use firm pressure on the top of your head if you are elderly, or suffering from epilepsy, bone disease, or clinical depression.

Step one
Start by scratching vigorously all over your head to loosen up your scalp. Then comb your fingers through your hair to remove any knots.

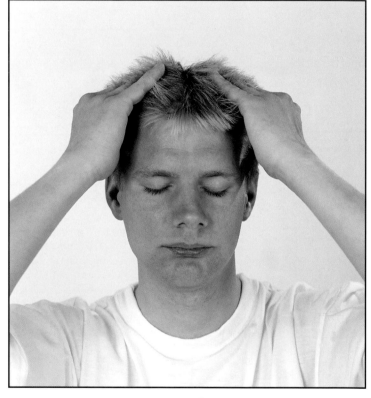

Step two
With your fingers apart, push your hands up into your hair, close to the scalp. Bring your fingers together to grip the hair and pull them out along its length. Hold for three to five seconds, then release. Repeat this pulling, moving your hands slightly each time, until you have covered your whole head.

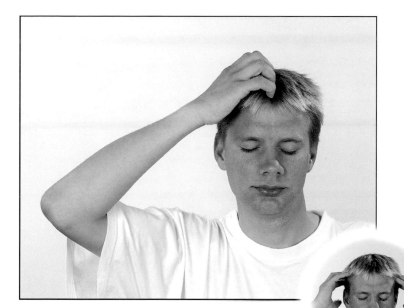

Step three

Place the pads of the fingers of one hand along the midline on the top of your head, with the little finger on the hairline and the others roughly 1cm (½in) apart. Rotate your fingers with firm pressure for 3–5 seconds. Move two fingerwidths back along the midline and repeat, continuing until you reach the base of the skull.

Now start again at the hairline and work lines two fingerwidths either side of the midline, using both hands at the same time. Continue in this way, finishing with a line just above the ears. End by rubbing vigorously all over your head.

Head sequence

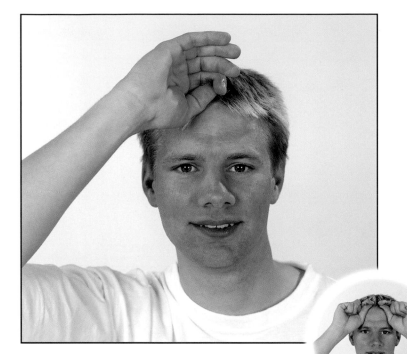

Step four

Starting at the hairline, in the middle of the forehead, take a small section of hair and pull gently for 3–5 seconds. If your hair is long enough, wrap a small twist around your finger to ensure an even tension. Release, move two fingerwidths back along the midline and repeat the process. Continue in this way until you reach the nape of the neck.

Return to the hairline and, using both hands, work two parallel lines two fingerwidths from the midline. When you reach the neck, run your fingers back up through the hair to ease out your scalp. Then work two more parallel lines back from the hairline. Repeat until you have covered your whole head.

Step five

Comb your fingers through your hair to loosen it. Place the fingertips of one hand along the midline on the top of the head, with your little finger on the hairline and fingers about 1cm (½in) apart. Press evenly and firmly for 3–5 seconds. Release and repeat, moving four fingerwidths backward each time, until you reach the nape of the neck.

Now start again at the hairline and work back across the head in parallel lines two fingerwidths from the first line, using both hands simultaneously. Try to work smoothly and rhythmically: imagine someone else is doing the work and all you have to do is enjoy it. Continue working parallel lines at two fingerwidth intervals until you reach your ears. Feel the tension draining away.

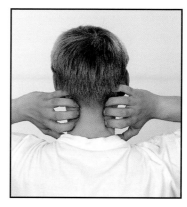

Step six

Pressure can release tension in a different way when worked from the back of your neck up toward the forehead. This time start at the base of the neck, with the fingers of both hands either side of the spine. Press as hard as you can into your neck and hold for about 5 seconds, then release. Move four fingerwidths up toward the crown and repeat, moving up the neck and on either side of the midline over the top of your head to the hairline.

Now return to the base of the neck and work two parallel lines two fingerwidths from the first. Repeat in this way until you have covered your whole head. Feel the tension lifting from your head.

Caution

Do not apply strong pressure directly on your spine.

Head sequence

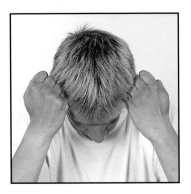

Step seven
Tap all over your head with the
fingertips of both hands. Your hands
should bounce off your hair lightly
and rhythmically.

Step eight
Loosely clench your fists and use
knuckling to work firmly over your
head. Starting at the base of the skull,
work from side to side across the
back of the head in parallel lines,
moving up two fingerwidths each
time. Then move to above your ears
and do the same on the sides of your
head. Finish with a firm knuckling over
the top of your head.

Step nine
Scratch your head vigorously all over
to complete the work on the scalp.

Ears sequence

There are many acupuncture points in the ears (see page 106). Using pressure and massage on these points balances the energy in your body and internal organs, and also in your mind and spirit. After this technique you may find your hearing is clearer and you feel brighter and more energetic.

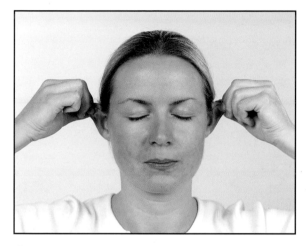

Step one
Start at the top of your ears, just where they join your head. Working on both ears simultaneously, pinch the outside ridge as hard as you can, pulling the ears away from your head, and massage slowly between finger and thumb for 3–5 seconds. Release, move one fingerwidth along the ridge, and repeat. Continue all round the outer edge of the ear.

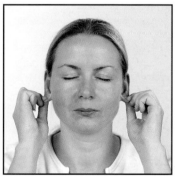

Step two
When you reach your ear lobes, grasp them firmly between index finger and thumb, pulling them down toward your shoulders for 3–5 seconds. Then pull the tops of your ears upward, also for 3–5 seconds.

Step three
Now move into your ears. Use your index finger inside and your thumb behind to pinch and massage all the ridges, nooks, and crannies as firmly as you can. Then work around the outer edge of the ear again, as in Step one.

Eyes sequence

Your eyes contain many muscles and giving them a regular workout can improve your sight. Short sight, long sight, astigmatism, and some focusing problems can all be helped by exercise and massage.

Step one
Start by holding your hands about 20cm (8in) in front of your face, with the palms facing each other 7cm (3in) apart. Be aware of the space between your hands and allow yourself to feel the flow of energy between your palms. Turn your palms to face you, slowly moving them closer to your eyes until you can sense the energy flowing into your eyes. Spend a moment or two with your eyes closed, feeling the strength of the energy flowing into them.

Step two
Still with your eyes closed, tense and relax the muscles within your eyes rhythmically for a count of 20. Then open your eyes and move your hands away from your face, holding one hand at full arm's length, the other about half way. Focus on one hand and then the other, moving quickly between them, for a count of 20.

Step three
Place your palms lightly over your eyes, taking care not to press on the lids. Feel the heat and energy from your palms relaxing your eyes. Tense and relax the muscles for a count of 20.

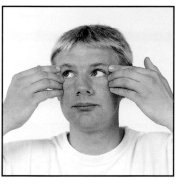

Step six
Place the tips of the four fingers of each hand beside the outer edge of the eyes, in a vertical line. Rotate them gently as you move your eyes down from the index to the little finger of one hand, and then the other. Repeat this slowly, five times. Finally, relax your eyes by placing your palms over them for 20 seconds, as in Step three.

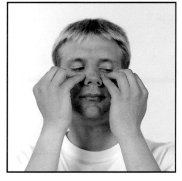

Step five
Place the tips of the four fingers of each hand in a line under your eyebrows and rotate gently. As you do so, move your eyes along from the tip of one index finger, along the other tips, to the other index finger, and back again. Repeat this slowly five times. Now move your fingers to underneath your eyes, just above the line of the cheekbone. Massage gently with rotations and move your eyes along the line of your fingertips, repeating five times, as before. Rest and relax your eyes by placing your palms over them for 20 seconds, as in Step three.

Step four
Gently massage the bridge of your nose for 2–3 seconds using one finger rotations (see page 19). Look at your finger as you massage, crossing your eyes. Work down the length of the nose and back up again in this way, moving one fingerwidth between positions and following your finger with your eyes. Repeat twice more. Then rest and relax your eyes by placing your palms over them for 20 seconds, as in Step three.

Face sequence

The next steps of the self-care routine work on the face, conditioning the facial muscles and promoting healthy teeth and gums. Facial massage also tones the internal organs and systems via the energy meridians and pressure points on the face (see page 106) and stimulates the lymphatic and endocrine systems (see page 107).

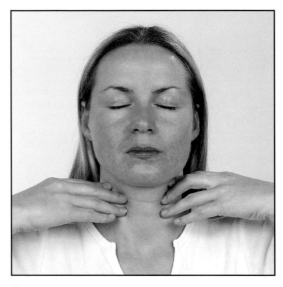

Caution
Do not massage the lymphatic areas on the sides of the face, the throat, across the chin, or behind the ears (see page 107), if you have cancer.

Step one
Start at the base of your throat, with your index, middle, and ring fingers in a horizontal line either side of your larynx. Rotate your fingers firmly for 3–5 seconds, then move up two fingerwidths and repeat. Continue up your throat and under your chin.

Caution
Do not massage your throat if you are pregnant.

Step two
Use your thumbs to make rotations with firm pressure under the jawbone, starting by the base of the ears. Rotate in one position for 3–5 seconds, then move two fingerwidths along the jawbone and repeat, until your thumbs meet in the middle under your chin.

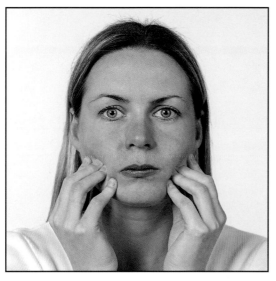

Step three

Next knead firmly along your bottom gums, using the four fingers of each hand. Start in front of your ears, massaging firmly down into the gum for 3–5 seconds and then moving two fingerwidths along the gum line to repeat. Continue until your hands meet on your chin.

Step four

Starting in front of your ears, knead along your top gum as in Step three, this time massaging up into the gum. Your hands should meet just under your nose.

Face sequence

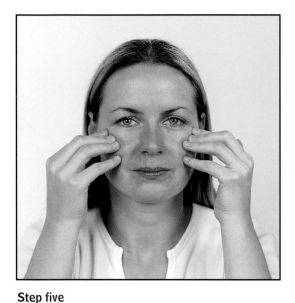

Step six
Use the index, middle, and ring fingers of both hands to rotate firmly in the hollow of your temples for 3–5 seconds.

Step five
Starting in front of the ears again, and using both hands simultaneously, use all four fingers to make light rotations along the cheekbones. Rotate for 3–5 seconds in each position, moving two fingerwidths along each time. Be very gentle under the eyes.

Step seven

Hold the four fingers of each hand so the tips are level and use them to tap firmly all over your face and throat. Work rhythmically with both hands together, keeping your wrists loose so the fingers bounce off your skin.

Caution

Do not massage your throat if you are pregnant.

Step eight

Place the four fingers of each hand on your forehead, in a horizontal line just below the hairline. Feel the muscles in your forehead beneath your fingers, and tense and release these 10 times. The movement is tiny: keep your eyebrows still. Move your fingers two fingerwidths down your face, tensing and releasing the muscles under your fingertips, until you have covered your whole face and throat.

With practice you will become more aware of these muscles and find it easier to tense them.

Gold ring visualization

When you have completed the self-care routine, gently rest your hands side by side on the top of your head with your elbows together in front of your face. Close your eyes and spend a few moments on this visualization, which will help to clear your aura, leaving you energized and refreshed.

You will need to record the words of the visualization first so that you can play them back as you relax.

Illness is believed to appear first in the aura, so using this visualization twice a day, with or without the head massage, will help you maintain good health and wellbeing.

Take a few deep breaths and visualize yourself floating in a clear night sky. Your aura surrounds you as a clear, bright light. Within this light there could appear grey or dark areas.

Move back until you can see the outer limits of your aura. It could be quite compact and close to your body, or it may spread out over a great distance. Make sure you can see it all.

Now see outside your aura a huge spinning gold ring, large enough to surround your aura. Within this ring is a fine gold mesh. As the ring comes toward you the mesh filters through your aura, collecting all the grey or dark patches of negative energy. You can feel yourself becoming lighter as these dark patches are drawn out.

When the gold ring has moved through and out of your aura, close it up with a lid and put another gold ring around it, to seal it. Then see it being taken far away from you into the universe, where the dense negative energy will be transformed into finer positive energy.

Look again at your aura. If there are any dark patches remaining, repeat the visualization until your aura is bright and glowing.

chapter four
Developing the senses

Strengthening your sensory perceptions through the techniques in this chapter will make you more aware, more creative, and happier in yourself and your environment.

Developing the senses

The meditations and visualizations in this chapter delve deeply into each area of sensory awareness in turn. Combined with light head massage, they help you develop your senses on a mental, emotional, and physical level. This increased sensory perception will open you to the awareness that everything you need is all around you all of the time – you don't have to cling fearfully to ideas, things, or people. Such an attitude blocks awareness of opportunities just waiting to happen, of people waiting to meet you, so you may miss chances that could enrich your life beyond your expectations.

The only massage technique used is a gentle stroking and touching near the relevant physical parts of your partner's head, while using a meditation or visualization to move her mind through various sensations. If you wish to work through the exercises on your own, record the words of the meditation first so you can concentrate on them completely.

You may want to use these treatments after carrying out the complete massage plan in chapter five, in which case you should move straight into the sense meditation before breaking the energy connection. Alternatively you can work on the senses only, treating one sense per session or combining them for a longer, deeper treatment. If you choose to work this way, omit the last step of each exercise, which brings your partner back to awareness of her surroundings, and continue until you have completed the whole treatment.

For each treatment, position yourself by your partner's head as she lies on the floor. Start by holding the head for a moment as you make the energy connection (see page 88). Talk your partner through the meditation or visualization in a slow, soft voice, allowing pauses between each step to allow her to relax deeply, and following the guidelines given in chapter two.

At the end of the meditation, remember to break the energy connection between you (see page 99).

Touch

Lightly stroke your partner's hair with alternate hands during this visualization.

Imagine you are walking by a river bank. Feel the path beneath your feet. Feel the warmth of the sun, the dappled coolness of the shady trees.

Sit down on the grass by the river. Feel the calming rhythms of the earth and the river.

Take off your shoes and put your bare feet into the cool water. Feel the watery coolness against your skin.

Run your hands over the grass and the riverside plants. Feel their different textures and shapes.

Put your feet on the river bottom. Feel the plants growing there, the small river-washed pebbles, the sharpness of the stones.

Sit for a while absorbing all these different textures, and the feelings and atmosphere of the river bank.

When you are ready, take your feet out of the water. Feel the movement of air against your wet feet. You are back in this room feeling revitalized and energized.

Taste

Before starting the visualization, spend five minutes on this exercise, which increases the sensitivity of touch and taste within the mouth and can also help improve tongue control for those with speech difficulties.

Ask your partner to breathe through her mouth. Lightly touch her cheek with your finger and ask her to touch her cheek in the same place inside the mouth with her tongue. Hold this position for a few moments while your partner explores all the sensations in the mouth – the feel, the taste, and the breath over her tongue. Move your finger to another position and repeat.

During the visualization, lightly stroke up the sides of the face from the chin to the temples.

Leave fairly long pauses between each step.

Imagine you are walking around a market.

You come to a baker's stall. You can smell the newly baked bread, pastries, and cakes. Sample everything on the stall, and enjoy the variety of tastes and textures.

Next you come to a stall selling herbs and spices. Smell their different aromas – ginger, mint, and cinnamon.

Taste any of the spices you wish.

Move on to the delicatessen stall and sample some exotic foods. Try spicy, sweet, sour, smoked, and pickled tastes.

The next stall sells all kinds of cheese. Try any you like – soft or hard, mild or strong.

Now, walking slowly, retrace your steps through the market. As you pass each stall imagine again all the tastes and textures you have tried.

Take a few deep breaths. As you breathe see if you can still taste all the different foods.

Now slowly come back to this room. Hold on to the richness of all you have tasted.

Smell

Using your index fingers alternately, lightly stroke down your partner's nose from the bridge to the tip during this meditation.

Imagine you are floating in a cloud. It can be any texture, color, or size you wish. If the cloud changes in any way, allow this to happen. Pay particular attention to the scents within the cloud.

First there is a heady smell of roses. It gets stronger and then as the cloud swirls around you, you become aware of other floral scents coming and going. You can choose the scent of any flower – rosemary, lavender, jasmine, sweet pea. Identify each one as it passes.

Other smells swirl around you in the cloud – the wood smoke from a bonfire, freshly cut grass, and damp, earthy smells. Be with each one as it comes and goes.

Now the cloud is full of the smells of foods: spices, coffee, sharp citrus fruits, freshly baked bread. Absorb these scents as they swirl past you.

Feel the changes in the cloud as all the different smells drift by. Enjoy each one. Allow them to come and go.

Pause and take a few deep breaths. Bring your partner's attention back to any scents in the room: aromatic oil, a burning candle, or a vase of flowers.

You are back in this room. Hold on to the variety of all the scents you have smelled.

Hearing

Lightly stroke down the outer ridge of your
partner's ears between your index finger and
thumb during this meditation.

Imagine you are lying under a shady tree
in the middle of a field in summer.

Around you are all the summer sounds
of life in this field.

Hear the wind in the leaves of the tree,
coming and going in soft gusty breaths.

Hear the songs of the many different kinds
of bird in the field.

Hear the insects, the crickets, the bees,
the busy life in the grass.

Hear the sound of water far away – a stream
splashing over pebbles, or perhaps a river
rushing over rocks.

Hear a plane buzzing high above you
in the sky.

Hear children playing happily in the field.

Hear the sounds of animals in the fields
nearby – cows, sheep, horses.

*Pause and take a few deep breaths. Bring your
partner's attention back to any sounds in the
room, such as a ticking clock.*

Hear the cars going past the window.
Hear my voice. You are back in this room
feeling refreshed and energized.

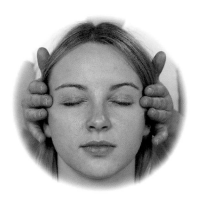

Sight

Slowly stroke the temples from the corner of the eyes to the hairline during this meditation.

See in front of you a beautiful flower.
It is tightly closed, its many layers of petals folded. You are going to open this flower with your breathing.

Breathe in and feel a golden light entering the top of your head.

Breathe out into the flower. The tight bud absorbs this golden light and the petals in the first layer open. They are a bright golden yellow.

Breathe in and now an orange light comes in through the top of your head.

Breathe out and the next layer opens. The petals glow orange.

Breathe in and the light changes to red.

The next layer opens. See and feel the glowing depth of color and energy in the red petals.

Breathe in. Now the light deepens to purple.

The purple layer of petals opens. Feel the healing qualities of this color.

Breathe in. The light changes to blue.

As the layer of blue petals opens, feel your energy lifting.

Breathe in. Now the light is turquoise.

The turquoise layer is now opening. Feel its protection.

Breathe in and a green light appears.

The green, regenerating layer opens.

Breathe in. The green light changes to a bright, golden yellow.

The central yellow petals open. Now the flower is fully formed.

Take a few moments to see and feel this rainbow of color. Feel its healing energy, its strength.

Now allow the flower to close gently within you. Take a few deep breaths, and come back to awareness of the room.

chapter five
Complete massage plan

This massage routine covers the whole head, neck, upper back, and shoulder areas, and is specifically designed to balance energy, tone the muscles, and release tension in the body.

Complete massage plan

The massage plan is given in two versions: one for the sitting position (pages 72–87); the other for lying down (pages 88–99). Each has full step-by-step instructions. Which you choose is up to you. Massage in the sitting position is more invigorating and stimulating for the receiver, while lying down allows the whole body to relax and re-energize.

Both versions of the plan have the same overall benefits for health and wellbeing. The differences in the steps accommodate the different positions of giver and receiver. Both versions tone the muscles and release stress and tension. By stimulating the body's energy meridians and pressure points the massage also balances energy in the internal organs, while stimulation of the lymphatic system boosts immunity, and the endocrine system balances the hormones. Where a step in the massage is particularly effective for certain conditions, this is noted in the description.

Given regularly, preferably once a week, the massage also has a cumulative beneficial effect on your mental state. Relaxation frees up your creativity, so you can deal with day-to-day problems and challenges more easily, and enables the body's own self-healing mechanism to work more effectively.

Both versions of the routine start with centering yourself (described opposite). Using the techniques described in chapter one, they begin with vigorous work on the neck, shoulders, and upper back before moving on to the slower and more meditative head massage. You should start to guide your partner through a meditation or visualization as you move on to the head sequence. Choose from the water meditation or leaf visualization at the end of this chapter, or the candle meditation (page 34) or cloud visualization (page 36) from chapter two.

To work through the complete massage plan will take about 30 to 40 minutes, though it may take longer the first couple of times, while you familiarize yourself with the steps. After massaging your partner you may wish to wait 15 to 20 minutes to ground yourselves before swapping roles.

Once you are confident with the steps of the routine, you can substitute any of the techniques from chapter one, following your intuition.

Caution
Observe the cautions on page 5.

Centering yourself

First prepare your surroundings: soften the lighting, play soothing music, burn essential oils (see page 13), and use the cleansing visualization on page 14 to clear negative energies. Now sit quietly for a few moments and use the golden light meditation on page 41 or the candle meditation on page 34 to center your energy. If you feel at all uncomfortable during the meditation take a break, then a few deep breaths, and start again. When working with a partner it is very important that your energies are harmonious and under control.

Sitting position

Sit your partner in a firm chair with low arms and back and stand squarely behind her.

Making the energy connection

Stand quietly with your thumbs together and palms facing downward, flat on the top of your partner's head. Allow your breathing to synchronize as you make contact with her energies. Close your eyes and visualize a pink healing light coming from the universe down into your head, flowing down your body into your energy center (two fingerwidths below your navel), and then flowing back up your body, along your arms, and through your hands into your partner. Watch this energy moving in a great circle from the heavens, through you both, down into the earth, and then back up to the stars. Try to maintain contact with this energy throughout the massage.

Upper back and shoulders sequence

Tension headaches and eye strain can originate between the shoulder blades, often as a result of poor posture while driving or using a computer, for example. Strong massage releases tension in this area before you start work on the head.

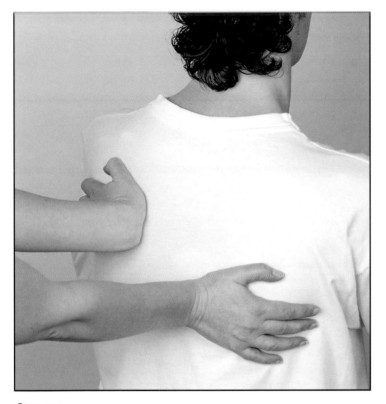

Caution

Do not apply strong pressure directly on the spine.

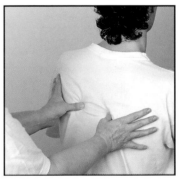

Step two
Place the pads of your thumbs either side of the spine, level with the lower edge of the shoulder blades. Leaning strongly on to your thumbs, make rotations for 3–5 seconds. Then move your thumbs out two fingerwidths and repeat, working along a horizontal line to the edge of the back. Start the next horizontal line beside the spine, two fingerwidths up from the first, and continue in this way up the back until you reach the neck.

Step one
Position the heels of your hands on either side of your partner's spine, level with the bottom of the shoulder blades. Lean your body weight on to your hands, pushing the muscles outward. Then creep (hand over hand) up the back, parallel to the spine, to the base of the neck, with your hands always in contact with the back. Repeat two or three times to loosen the tension in the upper back.

Upper back and shoulders sequence

Step three

Use strong thumb rotations with downward pressure at two fingerwidth intervals across the tops of the shoulders.

Caution

Do not massage the midpoint of the shoulders of anyone who is pregnant.

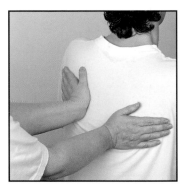

Step four

Starting with the heels of your hands either side of the spine and level with the bottom of the shoulder blades, lean and roll in across the heels, at the same time pushing the muscles outward. Work across the back in lines, up to the base of the neck, as in Step two.

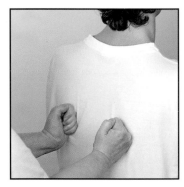

Step five

Clench your hands into fists and use strong pressure and a rolling action to knuckle up the upper back, pushing the muscles outward from the spine. You can work hand over hand all over one side and then the other, or else use both hands simultaneously to work in lines out from the spine over the whole upper back (see Step two).

Shoulders and upper arms sequence

Following the steps below helps to release locked or stiff muscles in the shoulder area, thus enabling the neck to move more freely. It also encourages deeper breathing.

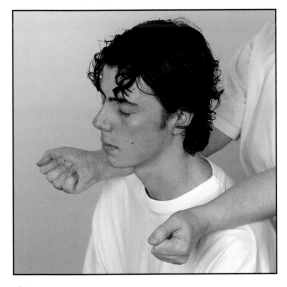

Step one

Place the backs of your forearms at the base of your partner's neck, on either side of the head. Your hands should face upward, fists loosely clenched. Lean down strongly for a count of five.

Now rock your body back, move your arms four fingerwidths away from the neck and lean down again. Repeat this action across the shoulders until you reach the tops of the arms.

Caution

Do not massage the midpoint of the shoulders of anyone who is pregnant.

Step two

From your position in Step one, rotate your forearms inward so your fists face each other. Keeping a strong pressure, slide your forearms down the outside of your partner's arms to the elbows. Repeat twice more, then rub all over the arms, back, and shoulders.

Neck sequence

Tension in the neck can aggravate headaches, eye strain, and focusing problems. Releasing this tension can relax the whole body.

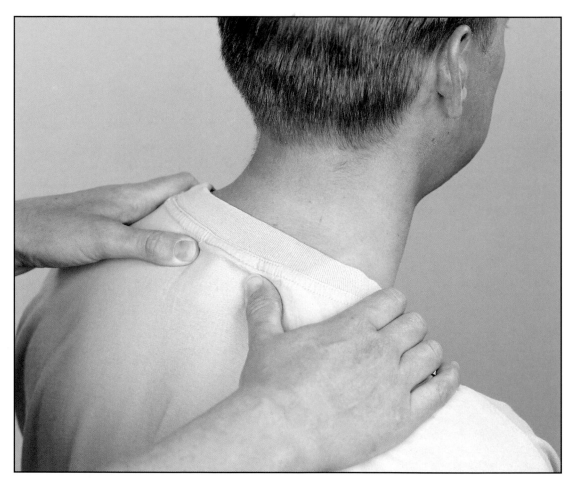

Step one
Place your hands on the shoulders with your thumbs either side of the spine at the base of the neck. Leaning your weight on to your thumbs, use thumb rotations to work up the neck on both sides of the spine, two fingerwidths from the midline, until you reach the base of the skull. Keep the pressure firm and even throughout. Repeat twice more.

Head sequence

Massage on the head releases tension in the scalp and improves blood circulation to the hair. Using these techniques slowly and rhythmically enables your partner to reach a very deep state of relaxation.

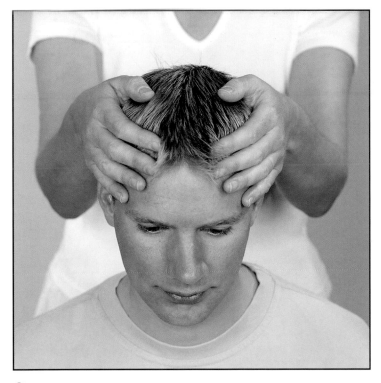

Caution

Do not use firm pressure on the top of the head on the very young, the elderly, or anyone suffering from epilepsy, bone disease, or clinical depression.

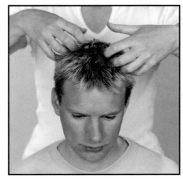

Step two

Stroke lightly all over your partner's hair with the palms of your hands. Then comb through the hair loosely with your fingers apart and relaxed, separating the hair but not touching the scalp. These soothing movements are used throughout the treatment to keep a smooth, flowing rhythm as you change from one technique to another.

Step one

With your hands on either side of your partner's head, hold the head lightly until your breathing synchronizes. This steadying action after the strong work on the shoulders and neck prepares you both for the more relaxing part of the massage routine. As you hold the position, re-establish your connection with the universal healing energy. Visualize a clear, bright light from far above you, passing through your body into your partner's body, and down into the earth.

Now start to talk your partner through the water meditation on page 100, or the leaf visualization on page 101.

Head sequence

Step three

Support the forehead with one hand, and use two fingers of the other hand to make rotations from the hairline back along the midline at one fingerwidth intervals. Work over the top of the head and down to the base of the skull. Here press upward with both fingers for a count of three. Return to the hairline and work a parallel line two fingerwidths from the first line. Finish by pressing upward at the base of the skull for a count of three. Continue until you have covered one side of the head. Stroke the hair for a few seconds, then change hands and repeat on the other side of the head.

Step four

Starting at the base of the skull, stroke and comb up through the hair toward the hairline, working over the scalp in the opposite direction to the rotations in Step three.

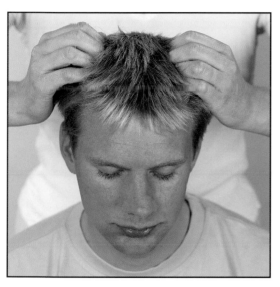

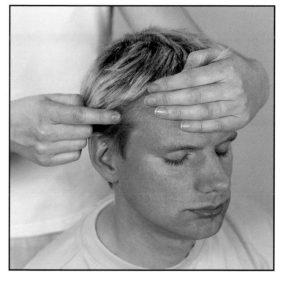

Step five

Hold your fingers with your nails in line and lightly scratch all over the head, keeping your wrists loose. This technique is invigorating and very good for skin conditions such as dandruff and psoriasis.
Stroke or comb through the hair for a few moments.

Caution

Do not work on broken skin, or sore areas of the scalp.

Step six

Support the head with one hand, and use one finger of the other hand to apply pressure for 3–5 seconds at one fingerwidth intervals along the midline. Start at the hairline and work back over the head to the nape of the neck, or work in the opposite direction if you prefer. Then work over one side of the head in the same way, in parallel lines two fingerwidths apart. Stroke the hair lightly and change hands to work on the other side of the head. This technique is excellent for heavy headaches, tension, and eye strain. Stroke or comb through the hair, from the nape of the neck to the hairline.

Head sequence

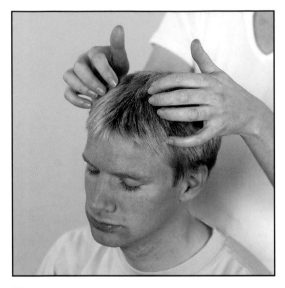

Step seven
Using both hands at the same time and keeping to a regular rhythm, tap all over the head. Keep your wrists loose and bounce off the scalp. This can be done lightly or vigorously, as your partner prefers.
Comb your fingers gently through the hair to remove any knots.

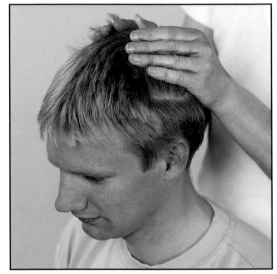

Step eight
Starting with your hands on either side of the neck, slide them up into the hair, fingers apart, keeping close to the scalp. When you have gathered a handful of hair, close your fingers firmly and pull away from the head. Allow the hair to move through your fingers under tension, creating a strong, even pull. Repeat all over the head, always pulling the hair at right angles away from the scalp.
Stroke or comb through the hair, from the nape of the neck to the hairline.

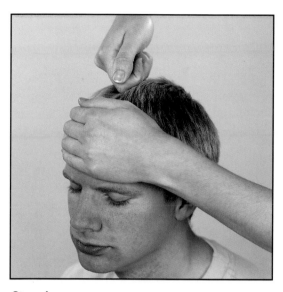

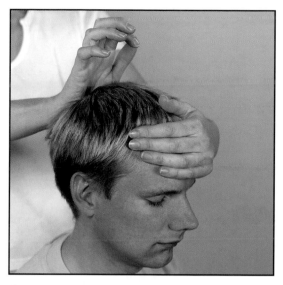

Step nine

Support the forehead with one hand. Make a fist with the other and knuckle up the neck and back of the head in a vertical line. Then work a parallel line, two fingerwidths from the first, over the side of the head. Stroke all over the hair, then change hands and repeat on the other side.

Step ten

Support the forehead with one hand. With the heel of the other hand, knead with strong pressure up the back of the neck and head to the crown. Then start at the neck again, this time kneading up over the side of the head. Stroke the hair as you change hands and knead up the neck and over the other side of the head. Then knead the top, from crown to forehead. Rub all over the head briskly, then gently comb or stroke the hair.

Throat sequence

Massage on the throat tones the neck muscles and also boosts the immune system by stimulating the lymphatic areas either side of the throat (see page 107).

Caution
Do not massage the throat of anyone who is pregnant or has cancer.

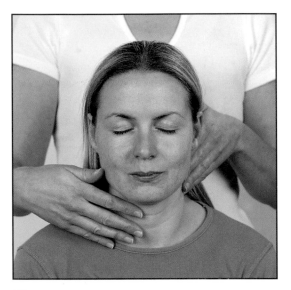

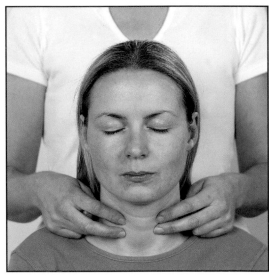

Step one
Rest your hands gently at the base of the throat for a moment or two. Reconnect with your partner's energies by visualizing the universal healing energy coming into your energy center, as on page 72. Now use your fingers to stroke up the throat and round under the ears, using alternate hands with brisk, light movements for about 30 seconds.

Step two
Working with both hands together, make two finger rotations gently up the throat, either side of the midline. Repeat on parallel lines two fingerwidths from the first. Then start under the chin and use four fingers to rotate firmly along the jawbone to the ears, moving two fingerwidths between rotations.

Face sequence

These techniques condition the facial muscles and promote healthy teeth and gums. Through the energy meridians, pressure points, and the lymphatic and endocrine areas on the face (see pages 105–107), face massage also tones and stimulates the internal organs, boosts the immune system, and balances the hormones. For these techniques use both hands on either side of the face simultaneously.

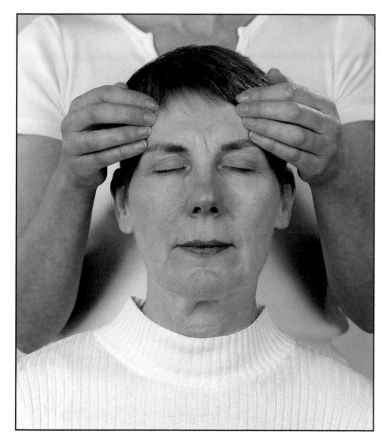

Caution

Do not massage the lymphatic areas on the sides of the face, the throat, across the chin, or behind the ears (see page 107), on anyone who has cancer.

Step one

With light, brisk finger movements, stroke up the sides of your partner's face from the jaw to the temples. Now work across the forehead with four finger rotations. Start in the middle with your fingertips in a vertical line and work outward with both hands, moving two fingerwidths between positions and rotating for 3–5 seconds on each point.

Face sequence

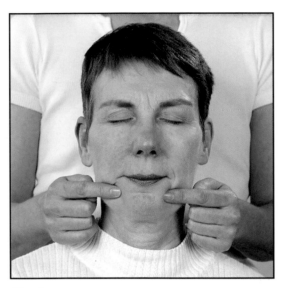

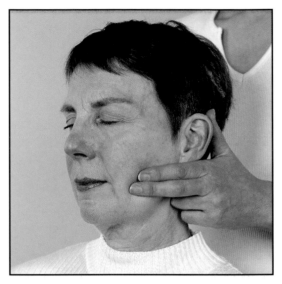

Step two

Starting in the middle of the chin, work along the jawbone with one finger rotations, one fingerwidth apart. Repeat in parallel lines at two fingerwidth intervals up over the cheeks, finishing on the cheekbones. Now return to the middle of the chin and use firm two finger pressure under the chin for 3–5 seconds. Repeat along the jawbone, moving two fingerwidths each time.

Step three

Use one or two fingers to knead along the lower gums, moving outward and back from the middle. Knead for 3–5 seconds in each position before moving two fingerwidths to the next. Then repeat along the upper gums. This technique stimulates blood flow to the gums and encourages healthy teeth.

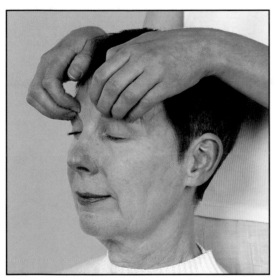

Step four
Hook all four fingers gently under the cheekbones and hold this position for 3–5 seconds. Then do the same under the eyebrows.

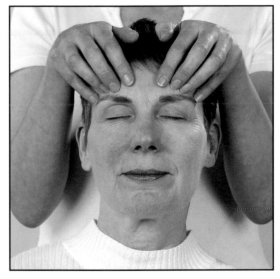

Step five
Now apply firm pressure into the skull with all four fingers on the forehead, just above the eyebrows.
These techniques help sinus conditions and can lift heavy headaches.

Ears sequence

Massage on the ears balances energy in the body, mind, spirit, and the internal organs through stimulation of the acupuncture points illustrated on page 106. Use both hands for these techniques, to work on both ears simultaneously.

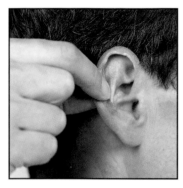

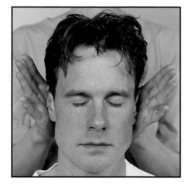

Step one
Starting at the top of the ears where they meet the head, and pinching between index finger and thumb, rotate all around the outer edge. When you reach the lobes, pinch them firmly and pull them down toward the shoulders for 3–5 seconds.

Step two
Rub the ears briskly then cup your hands over them for 3–5 seconds. They will probably be quite hot and your partner may hear a ringing or buzzing sound, which should fade after a few moments.

Breaking the energy connection

Finish the treatment by holding your partner's head firmly but gently with your hands on either side. Visualize the clear white light of healing energy flowing down from the universe into your head, through you and your partner, down into the earth, and back up again to the stars, in a huge circle.

Now see this flow of white light being cut above your head. Remove your hands from your partner, holding them 2–3cm (1–1½in) above her head. See the light flowing down through your body, through your partner, out through the bottom of your feet, and into the earth. Step back and stamp your feet, breathing deeply to ground yourself. This breaks the energy connection between you.

Lying down

Thoroughly pad the floor with a duvet, sleeping bag, or folded blankets. Your partner should lie on her back for the massage. Make sure you have some padding to sit on too. Kneel or sit on the floor above and close to your partner's head, so that you can comfortably reach down the back of her neck and under her shoulders.

These back, neck, and shoulder techniques can be replaced with the techniques from the sitting position section of this chapter if you prefer.

Making the energy connection

Sit quietly with your hands resting either side of your partner's head. Allow your breathing to synchronize as you make contact with her energies. Close your eyes and visualize a pink healing light coming from the universe down into your head, flowing down your body into your energy center (two fingerwidths below your navel), and then flowing back up your body, along your arms, and through your hands into your partner. Watch this energy moving in a great circle from the heavens, through you both, down into the earth, and then back up to the stars. Try to maintain contact with this energy throughout the massage.

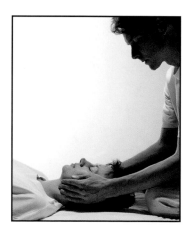

Upper back and shoulders sequence

Tension headaches and eye strain can originate between the shoulder blades, often as a result of poor posture while driving or using a computer, for example. Strong massage releases tension in this area before you start work on the head.

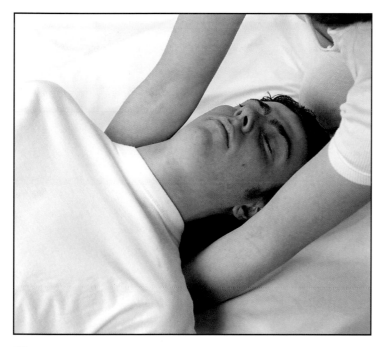

Step two
Use the heels of your hands to knead across the tops of the shoulders, from the neck outward to the top of the arms, and back again.

Caution
Do not massage the midpoint of the shoulders of anyone who is pregnant.

Step one
Holding your hands flat, with the palms facing upward, reach down under your partner's back as far as you can. Make a claw shape with your hands, then start next to the spine and move both hands out toward the sides in a horizontal line.
Your partner's body weight increases the pressure in this powerful technique. If you can, repeat twice more in parallel lines two fingerwidths apart.

Neck sequence

Tension in the neck can aggravate headaches, eye strain, and focusing problems. Releasing this tension can relax the whole body.

Caution
If you have a history of neck problems you should consult your doctor before using this sequence.

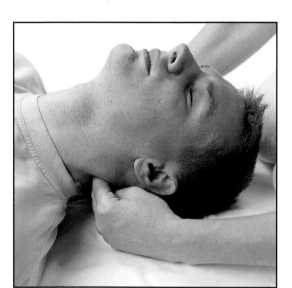

Step one
Hold your hands together under the base of the neck, so that it rests on your index fingers. Keeping your hands together, pull strongly upward and toward the nape of the neck. Repeat twice more.

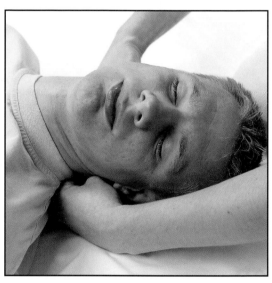

Step two
With your hands in the same position as Step one, change to a hand over hand action, still pulling in the same direction. This rolling movement will rock the head gently from side to side. Continue for a count of 20, to loosen the neck muscles.

Hold the back of your partner's neck until your breathing synchronizes. As you hold the position, re-establish your connection with the universal healing energy by visualizing a clear, bright healing light from far above you in the universe passing through your body, into your partner's body, and down into the earth.

Now start to talk your partner through the water meditation on page 100, or the leaf visualization on page 101.

Head sequence

Massage on the head releases tension in the scalp, and improves blood circulation to the hair. Using these techniques slowly and rhythmically enables your partner to reach a very deep state of relaxation.

Caution
Do not use firm pressure on the top of the head on the very young, the elderly, or anyone suffering from epilepsy, bone disease, or clinical depression.

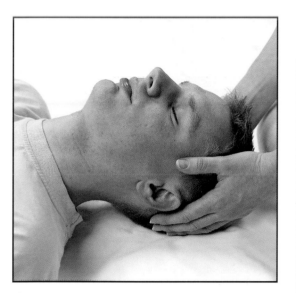

Step one
Gently stroke upward all over your partner's hair. This soothing movement is used throughout the treatment to keep a smooth, flowing rhythm as you change from one technique to another.

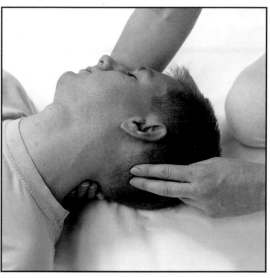

Step two
Turn your partner's head to one side and support the neck with one hand, letting the head rest on your forearm. Work a line up the middle of the back of the neck and head to the crown, using two finger rotations with one finger either side of the midline. Rotate for 3–5 seconds at each point, moving two fingerwidths between points. Work a second line two fingerwidths from the first, up the neck, and over the side of the head.
Now turn the head to the other side and repeat the two finger rotations up the midline and then over the side of the head.

Head sequence

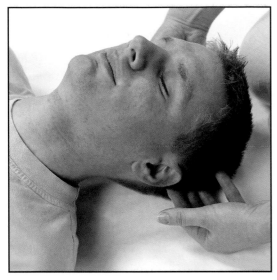

Step three
Turn your partner's head to the front and slide your hands under the back of the head as far as you can reach. Work up the sides of the head to the temples, using four finger rotations at two fingerwidth intervals.

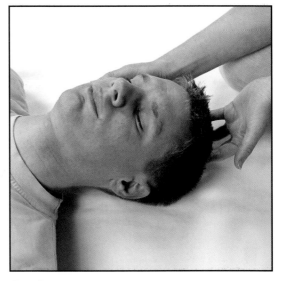

Step four
Now support the side of the head and use the four fingers of one hand to make rotations over the top of the head in one big sweep from the crown to the forehead. Gently stroke or comb through the hair for a few moments.

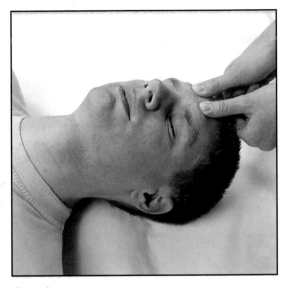

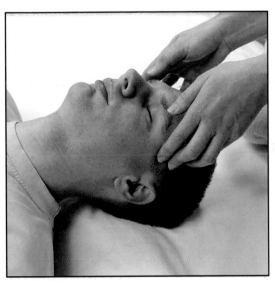

Step five
Slide your hands under the back of the head as far as you can reach. Use the four fingers of one hand to press firmly for 3–5 seconds. Work up the sides of the head in this way, moving two fingerwidths between positions and finishing at the temples.

Step six
Starting at the temples, use firm thumb pressure to work a line in across the middle of the forehead, holding each position for 3–5 seconds and moving one fingerwidth to the next. Finish where your thumbs meet in the middle.

Head sequence

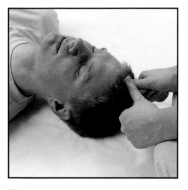

Step seven
With your thumbs overlapping, use thumb pressure to work a line from the middle of the forehead down to the crown. Hold the pressure for 3–5 seconds on each point and move back two fingerwidths between positions. Then use one thumb on each side of the head to work two lines, two fingerwidths from, and parallel to, the first line; then on two lines from the "corners" of the forehead. Gently stroke or comb through the hair for a few moments.

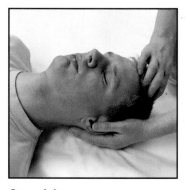

Step eight
Starting as far toward the back of the head as you can reach, scratch lightly all over the scalp, keeping your wrists loose so that the movement is light, free, and flowing.

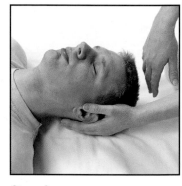

Step nine
Use the four fingers of both hands to tap all over the head, starting as far back as you can reach and moving up over the sides. Try to work in regular lines, and keep your wrists loose so your fingertips bounce off the head. Work either lightly or vigorously, as your partner prefers. Then support the head and tap over the top, from crown to forehead and back again, using the backs of the fingers. Comb through the hair with your fingers to loosen any knots or tangles.

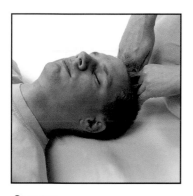

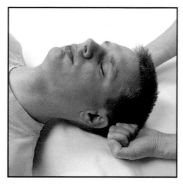

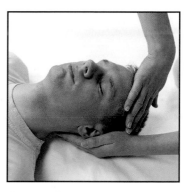

Step ten

Turn your hands so that the palms face outward, spread your fingers, and push them down through the hair at the sides of the head. When you have gathered a handful of hair, close your fingers to grip it and then pull slowly away from the head, letting the hair move through your fingers under tension. Repeat this step in a smooth, flowing manner all over the head, always pulling the hair at right angles to the scalp.

Step eleven

Starting as far down the back of the head as you can reach, knuckle up and over both sides of the head at the same time, finishing at the temples. Then support the head with one hand while you knuckle over the top with the other, rolling across the knuckles from side to side and moving forward from the crown to the forehead.

Step twelve

Knead simultaneously up both sides of the head to the temples, so the pressure from each hand balances the other. Use an open hand, and knead with pressure from the heel of the palm to the base of the fingers. Then support the head with one hand and knead over the top with the other, as for knuckling in Step eleven.

Face sequence

These techniques condition the facial muscles and promote healthy teeth and gums. Through the energy meridians, pressure points, and the lymphatic, and endocrine areas on the face (see pages 105–107), face massage also tones and stimulates the internal organs, boosts the immune system, and balances the hormones. For these techniques use both hands on either side of the face simultaneously.

Caution

Do not massage the lymphatic areas on the sides of the face, the throat, across the chin, or behind the ears (see page 107), on anyone who has cancer.

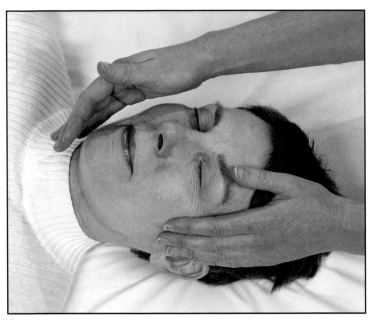

Step one
Using alternate hands, stroke up the throat and sides of the face toward the temples in a continuous motion. Do this for 10 seconds, then stroke very lightly with the fingertips from the chin up to the cheekbones, and then on the forehead, avoiding the eyes.

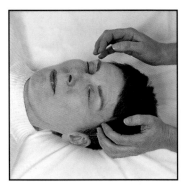

Step two
Use the four fingers of both hands to tap lightly up the throat and over the face toward the temples.

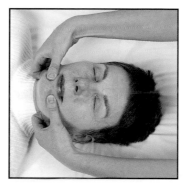

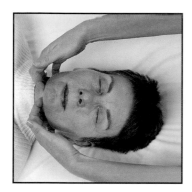

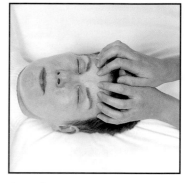

Step three

Hook four fingers under each eyebrow and press gently with the fingertips for 3–5 seconds. Release, then hook under the cheekbones in the same way and press again. Then do the same under the jawbone, with your index fingers together under the chin and your other fingers spread out along the jaw.

Step four

Use your thumbs to knead along the lower gum, starting at the back of the jaw and meeting under the middle of the lower lip. Knead each position for 3–5 seconds, before moving one fingerwidth to the next. Then repeat along the upper gums. This technique stimulates blood flow to the gums, and encourages healthy gums and teeth. Stroke the face lightly with your fingertips. Work from the middle out to the ears, on the forehead, beside the nose, and on the chin.

Step five

Start with the four fingers of both hands in a horizontal line across the base of the throat. Rotate gently for 3–5 seconds, then move up two fingerwidths and repeat, until you reach the chin.

Now start at the jawbone and continue using four finger rotations up the cheeks to the temples. Then start again above the eyebrows and use four finger rotations to work up the forehead to the hairline. Use light pressure without pulling the skin. Stroke gently with your fingertips up both sides of the face to finish.

Ears sequence

Massage on the ears balances energy in the body, mind, spirit, and the internal organs through stimulation of the acupuncture points illustrated on page 106. Use both hands for these techniques, to work on both ears simultaneously.

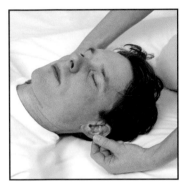

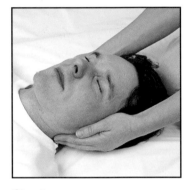

Step one
Starting at the top of the ears where they meet the head, and pinching between index finger and thumb, rotate all around the outer edge. When you reach the lobes, pinch them firmly and pull them down toward the shoulders for 3–5 seconds.

Step two
Rub the ears briskly, then cup your hands over them for 3–5 seconds. They will probably be quite hot and your partner may hear a ringing or buzzing sound, which should fade after a few moments.

Breaking the energy connection

Finish the treatment by holding your partner's head firmly but gently with your hands on either side. Visualize the clear white light of healing energy flowing down from the universe into your head, through you and your partner, down into the earth, and back up again to the stars, in a huge circle.

Now see this flow of white light being cut above your head. Remove your hands from your partner, holding them 2–3cm (1–1½in) above her head. See the light flowing down through your body, through your partner, out through the bottom of your feet, and into the earth. Move back away from your partner. Take some deep breaths and shake your hands vigorously. This breaks the energy connection between you.

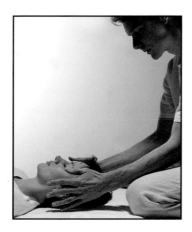

Water meditation

This meditation allows your partner to reach a state of deep relaxation while you work at a slow, meditative pace. Speak in a slow, soft, gentle but firm voice.

Vary the pauses between sentences so that you reach the long pause as you begin to massage the ears.

Be aware of your breathing. Feel your breath gently moving into your body and back out again.

Feel your breath slowly filling your whole body each time you inhale.

Feel the tension in your muscles leaving your body each time you exhale.

Breathe in. Feel your body becoming softer and softer.

Breathe out. Feel your body slowly dissolving.

You are becoming lighter and more fluid with each breath.

See yourself glowing with a soft rainbow colored light.

Your body is becoming lighter, you are floating. Your body is spreading out, you are becoming like the surface of a lake.

As the lake is blown by the warm breeze, the sun creates tiny rainbows within the ripples.

Stay with this feeling of liquid, light, and color. Let these feelings develop. Allow any changes in your body and mind to happen.

Long pause…

As you come to the end of the massage, start speaking again.

Now feel your body becoming more dense. You are becoming yourself once more.

Feel your body re-forming, bringing with it the power and energy of the water, colors, and the sun.

Now you should be at the end of the treatment, holding your partner's head as you break the energy connection between you.

Take a few deep breaths and come back to awareness.

Leaf visualization

This is an excellent grounding visualization which can help to stabilize an over energetic mind and body. While you work, imagine you are also within this visualization and simply describe everything that happens to you. This script is only a guide.

Vary the pauses between sentences so that you reach the long pause as you begin to massage the ears.

Take a few breaths to center yourself.

As you observe the air moving in and out of your body, feel yourself spreading out, becoming very light, very flexible, boneless.

Feel yourself drifting in a cool breeze. You are very loose. You are being wafted up and down, from side to side. You are so light you are being carried by the gentlest of air currents.

Feel yourself moving like a leaf on the topmost branch of a tall tree.

Look down and see the ground far below. Enjoy floating in the air with just the faintest connection between you, the tree, and the earth.

Now put your awareness into that connection. The stem joining you to the tree brings you life, strength, and power.

Feel the power of all living things moving through you.

Feel the power of the tree drawing you toward it.

Feel the hard, woody texture of the tree as you become part of it.

You are becoming stronger as you move into the branch.

You are moving along the branch and into the trunk of the tree, absorbing the strength and vitality of the tree and the earth beneath.

Feel every sensation – the flow of energy, health, power. You are being reconstructed as you feel the power of life growing within you.

Long pause…

Now you should be at the end of the treatment, holding your partner's head as you break the energy connection between you.

Now slide down the tree, and out on to the ground. Be aware of your breathing. Feel yourself coming back to reality. Start to be aware of your surroundings as you return, feeling strengthened and regenerated.

chapter six

Treating common ailments

The step-by-step treatment plans in this chapter show you how
to use the power of head massage to promote healing for
25 common ailments and conditions.

Treating common ailments

The plans in this chapter give a comprehensive general treatment for 25 ailments and conditions, working on the channels and areas illustrated on the following pages. Refer back to these illustrations as you follow the treatment plans.

The exact position of channels, areas, and points varies from person to person, therefore the illustrations should be used as a guide.

Channels

The free and balanced flow of energy in mind, body, and spirit maintains good health. This energy flows along channels that are related to the body's organs or functions. Massage on these channels frees blocked energy, balancing energy flow in the related organ system.

Most of the channels occur in pairs, symmetrically on either side of the body. Not all of them extend as far as the head, but some, such as the lung channel, have an extension channel in the neck and head area which can be treated in the same way as the channel itself.

In the treatment plans in this chapter you will notice that some massage points seemingly unrelated to the problem are used to stimulate the healing process. For example, respiratory problems respond to massage on the bladder channel. This is because the respiratory system is part of a vast network that deals with elimination. This includes the digestive system, blood circulation, bowels, bladder, tears, sweat, nail and hair growth, skin and cellular replacement at all levels, and even emotions. If there is a problem in the respiratory system, stimulating other systems concerned with elimination, such as the bladder, takes the pressure off the weakened respiratory system, allowing it to recover.

Key

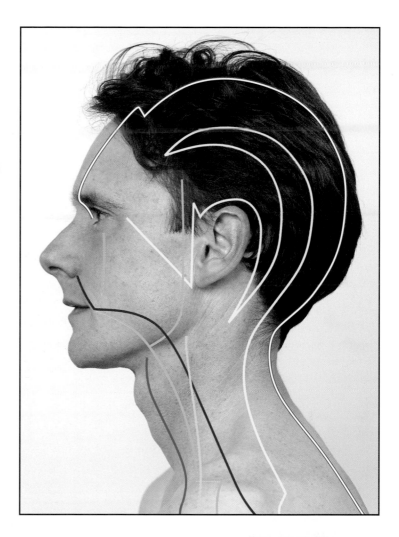

■ large intestine channel

▦ stomach channel

▦ spleen extension channel

  gall bladder channel

■ lung extension channel

☐ bladder channel

Still points

Along the base of the skull are still points which can be used to slow the heart rate, deepen breathing, lower blood pressure, assist with lymph drainage, and deeply relax the body. Since lymph can transport some forms of cancer cells around the body, these areas should not be massaged on anyone who has cancer.

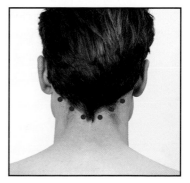

Pressure areas on the face

Some areas on the face relate to specific organs, for example the pancreas points, which are located either side of the middle of the chin. Massage on these areas tones and balances the related organ system.

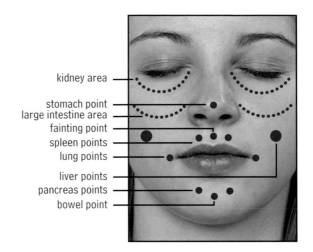

kidney area
stomach point
large intestine area
fainting point
spleen points
lung points
liver points
pancreas points
bowel point

Pressure points in the ears

Acupuncturists use over 200 points in the ears to treat all parts of the body and mind. Treating these with pressure, as in finger and thumb massage, is known as acupressure. Since fingers and thumbs are quite blunt instruments, massaging in the ears allows you to stimulate several points at once.

Massaging all over the ears benefits the whole being, regulating the digestive system, improving immunity, clearing the breathing, lowering blood pressure, and detoxifying.

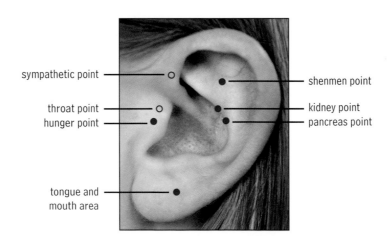

sympathetic point
throat point
hunger point
tongue and mouth area
shenmen point
kidney point
pancreas point

The endocrine system

The body responds to stressful situations by releasing hormones such as adrenaline and cortisol. Massage on the endocrine areas (see right) stimulates the pineal, pituitary, and thyroid glands to balance hormone levels. This helps to counteract the negative effects of stress, which is a major component of many ailments and conditions.

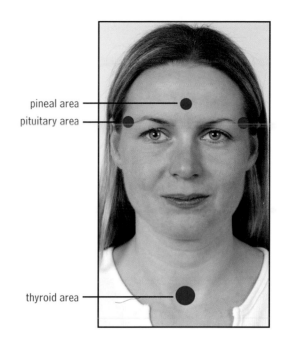

pineal area

pituitary area

thyroid area

The lymphatic system

Lymph (a clear fluid) travels through the body via the lymphatic system, clearing toxins. It is a major component of the immune system, so massaging the lymphatic areas on the sides of the face, the throat, across the chin, and behind the ears, strengthens immunity. Since lymph can transport some forms of cancer cells around the body, these areas should not be massaged on anyone who has cancer.

Balancing the body's energies

General head, neck, and shoulder massage is a wonderful way to relax and de-stress the body, mind, and spirit. Since stress imbalance aggravates almost every ill, relaxing and balancing stress levels promotes general wellbeing. In addition to stress overload, many ailments are also greatly aggravated by the build-up of toxins within the body, energy and hormone imbalances, and reduced immunity.

Relaxing mind and body enables the self-healing mechanisms to work at maximum efficiency. Detoxing frees more energy for cellular repair and regeneration. Your skin becomes clearer, you feel more alive, your mind and body feel more in tune and energized.

The treatment plans in this chapter all include relaxation and detox techniques relevant to the particular ailment being treated, in addition to other beneficial massage steps and a visualization that specifically promotes healing of the condition. You can follow these plans to treat yourself, though the treatment will be more effective if a partner gives you the massage, thus allowing you to concentrate fully on the visualization. All the treatments are safe to use on both adults and children, though you should only ever use a light touch on the very young or elderly, and observe the cautions given on page 5. Always start by working through the complete massage plan in chapter five, stopping just before you break the energy connection with your partner, and then continuing with the appropriate treatment plan.

Treating ailments

The techniques for treating ailments and conditions work on the channels and areas illustrated on pages 105 to 107. However, many different points and channels can be massaged to achieve the same result, and some may work better than others, depending on the individual. Also, people have their own preferences – some do not like having their faces massaged, others may have extra sensitivity in the neck or throat. Once you feel confident with the steps suggested, if you feel that your partner would benefit from work on a particular area, or that a particular massage technique would be more effective, go with it. Work

Caution
The treatments in this chapter are safe and effective but are not intended to replace the care of a qualified medical practitioner. Do not make any changes to your existing treatment or medication without consulting your doctor. Observe the cautions on page 5.

intuitively, with love and care and a desire for the wellbeing of others, and you will give more healing than if you try to stick to a regimented format.

During the treatment it is important to keep the energy moving. Otherwise, although you may damp down the symptoms, a build-up of energy may cause a blockage, which could lead to problems later. Visualize a white, violet, or pink light around the problem while you work. At the end of the session, as you break the energy connection between you, see this light flowing down your partner's body, out of the soles of the feet, and away into the universe.

The healing crisis

When you use head massage treatments you may find you seem to get worse before you get better. This is because the therapy is getting to the root of the problem, not merely suppressing the symptoms.

Delving into a problem can disturb a lot of deeply buried discomfort and can also reveal emotional pain. Experiencing a release in body or mind, pain, or dreaming and reliving past events are fairly common reactions to treatment.

Many people give up at this point, preferring to leave the discomfort as quickly as possible. Stick with it if you can, and use the pain to clear out deep-seated problems. You can then rise beyond your old self into a new, positive, creative, energetic, and exciting you.

Detox

Toxins in our everyday environment can include pollutants in the air, pesticides on our food, and chemicals in cleaning products. Natural substances can also be toxins: too much fat or sugar in a rich meal, or too much alcohol. Stress reduces the body's natural ability to cope with such toxins, and signs of toxic overload may include skin or hair problems and other minor ailments.

These treatments stimulate the elimination systems to rid the body of toxins and balance the hormonal system. Many of the treatments in this chapter include this detox routine, since reducing toxins allows the body's healing mechanism to cope with the underlying cause of the illness.

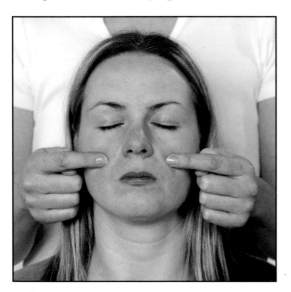

▲ **Step one**
Use finger rotations along the stomach and large intestine channels (see page 105). Rotate firmly and slowly on each position for 10–30 seconds, moving back two fingerwidths each time. Massage in the same way along the bladder channel (see page 105).

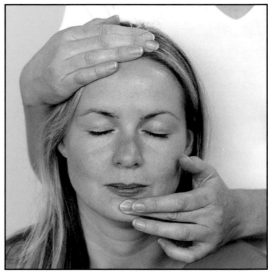

▲ **Step two**
The midpoint of the chin is the bowel point (see page 106). Massage here for 10–30 seconds with firm thumb rotations. Then use finger rotations on the end of the nose (the stomach point, see page 106) for 10–30 seconds.

Visualization

Visualize a white light coming down through the top of your head. Slowly it fills your head, neck, shoulders, arms, and hands. Now the light moves into your body, filling all the organs, then down into your legs and out through the soles of your feet. Feel this light flowing in a continuous movement through your body, picking up grey areas of negative energy, and moving them out through the soles of your feet, down into the earth.

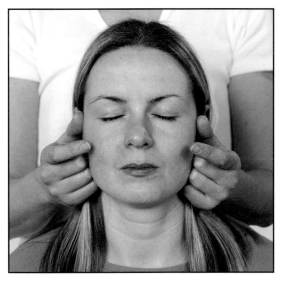

▲ Step three
Put your index finger in the ear, with the edge of the nail aligned with the ear hole. Slide it up until it meets the inner ridge and then rock the finger back: the pad of the finger will now be on the kidney and pancreas points (see page 106). Massage with pressure for 10–30 seconds to stimulate the kidneys and regulate salt and sugar levels in the blood.

▲ Step four
Tap gently with one finger around the eye sockets below the eye, from the nose around to the outer corner. This area relates to the kidneys, bowels, and large intestine. Then use firm finger rotations, pressure, and tapping over the middle of the forehead, the temples, and the base of the throat, to balance the endocrine system.

Headaches

The most common cause of headache is tension, which often originates in the shoulders, leading to tight muscles in the neck and scalp. Sinus problems may cause head pain across the forehead and cheeks. Bilious headaches may result from overeating, or too much rich food or drink. Regular head massage relaxes the shoulders, neck, and head.

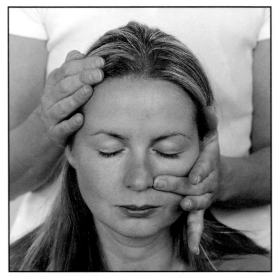

▲ Treatment one

For tension headaches, use strong scalp, neck, and shoulder massage. Starting on the shoulders, work up the neck and all over the scalp, using thumb rotations, heel of hand kneading, pressure, hacking, hair pulling, and tapping. This loosens tight muscles and releases pain.

Hair pulling can also be very effective for this type of headache. As you work over the scalp you may find painful hot spots. Grasp the hair over the affected area and hold it under tension for 10–20 seconds, then release. This relaxes the muscles of the scalp and can make a headache vanish in seconds.

▲ Treatment two

For sinus headaches, massage either side of the nostrils with the pad of your middle finger, resting it under the cheekbones. Apply firm pressure along the length of the finger for 5–10 seconds, then use rotations at one fingerwidth intervals. Follow this with finger pressure along the cheekbones, holding for 5–10 seconds before moving along one fingerwidth to the next point. You can also use finger pressure on the middle of the bridge of the nose. This is particularly useful if the cheekbones are tender.

Caution

Do not use these techniques on anyone who has had surgery to drain the sinuses.

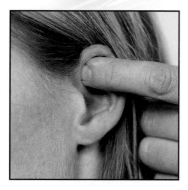

▲ Treatment three

To lift a fuzzy headache and to relieve any head pain, massage the sympathetic point on the ear (see page 106). This is near the top of the ear, close to where it joins the head. Slide your finger under the outer ridge and press on the inner end of the horizontal ridge. Your partner should breathe deeply as you massage this area as you will find her mind clears very quickly.

Treatment four

To clear toxins, use the detox massage treatment plan on pages 110–111.

Visualization

Imagine a gold ring spinning and encircling your body around your energy center (two fingerwidths below your navel). Allow it to rise up your body, and up from the top of your head, moving the pain with it, up and out of your body.

Migraine

Migraine headaches result from tension and physical stress in the membrane around the brain and the muscles of the scalp. Causes of such tension may include stress, eyestrain, hormone imbalances, infection, neck and back problems, allergy, excesses of food or alcohol, and depression.

Do not use head massage during an attack, as it can intensify the discomfort. Instead, use these treatments once or twice a week as a preventive measure, to reduce the frequency of attacks.

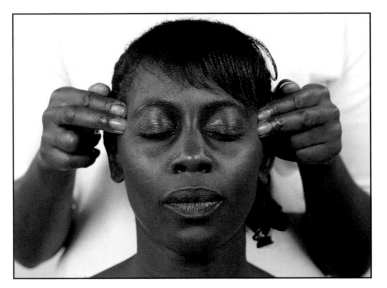

Visualization

Imagine lying under a lime tree in early spring. The day is warm and you can see the sky through the pale green and yellow leaves. The blues, yellows, and greens flow through you, draining away all tension and pain.

▲ Treatment one
To balance the endocrine system, massage the middle of the forehead (pineal gland), the temples (pituitary), and base of the throat (thyroid) with two finger rotations for 10–30 seconds on each. If your partner finds rotations too strong, use stroking instead.

Treatment two
To release tension in the scalp and membrane around the brain, use stroking, rotations, and light pressure all over the head, working in regular lines. Then work horizontal lines on the neck, shoulders, and upper back with kneading and strong thumb rotations. Finish by tapping lightly over all these areas.

Treatment three
To clear toxins, use the detox massage treatment plan on pages 110–111.

Neuralgia

This localized nerve pain commonly affects the cheek and gum areas, but may also occur in the throat and ears, or on other areas of the body, for example with shingles. Other possible causes are stress, emotional upset, vitamin deficiencies, and excess alcohol.

Massage affected areas daily to reduce pain. If you suffer recurrent attacks, use these techniques twice a week until the incidence is reduced, then weekly as a preventive measure.

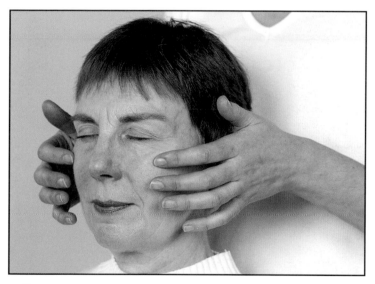

Visualization

Feel your head surrounded by a bright yellow cloud. Ice-blue shards move through the cloud. When one comes close, feel its coolness drawing the pain away. As the pain drifts away, the ice melts and the blue and yellow mingle. Stay with this calming, healing, pale green colour.

▲ Treatment one

To relieve pain, use rotations and pressure to massage firmly in lines across the forehead from the middle out to the temples. Then work along the cheekbones to the bridge of the nose using tapping or rotations. Massage each point for 10–30 seconds before moving to the next. Stroke lightly from the middle of the forehead to the temples, then back along the cheekbones to the nose. Treat other affected areas similarly.

Treatment two

To release tension in the facial muscles, massage the back of the neck with strong thumb rotations, working out from either side of the spine in horizontal lines.

Treatment three

To clear toxins, use the detox massage treatment plan on pages 110–111.

Sleep disturbance

Problems with sleeping have many causes, including emotional disturbance, digestive problems, allergies, and overstimulation, for example from watching television last thing before bed.

Working through the complete massage plan twice a week calms and reduces stress, helping the mind to organize information. Use once a week when symptoms improve.

Treatment one
Strong thumb rotations up the back of the neck will help to relax the mind. To release tension across the shoulders, firmly knead the upper back and shoulders with the heels of the hands, then follow with thumb rotations and pressure. In both these areas work in lines out from the middle, massaging for 10–30 seconds on each point.

▲ Treatment two
Calm the mind by massaging the shenmen point in the ear (see page 106). This is on the edge of the dimple just below the outer ridge at the top of the ear, at this dimple's furthest point from the head. Pinch firmly with your thumb behind the ear and finger inside and massage with rotations for 10–30 seconds.

▲ Treatment three
To slow down mind and body and coax your partner into relaxed sleep, use light rotations slowly and repetitively on the endocrine areas: the middle of the forehead, the temples, and base of the throat (see page 107).

Visualization

Feel yourself floating high in the sky as the sun is setting. The sky is filled with yellows, oranges, purples, and pinks. Feel the warm air all around. As the sky darkens and the blue deepens, feel yourself falling into a calm, restful sleep.

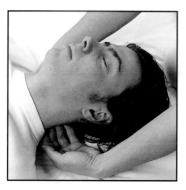

Caution
Do not massage these areas on anyone who has cancer.

▲ Treatment four
Massage with upward stroking, four finger rotations, and pressure in lines over the lymphatic areas on the throat, under the jaw, the sides of the face, and the back of the neck (see page 107).

Treatment five
To clear toxins, use the detox massage treatment plan on pages 110–111.

Hyperactivity

This condition can be aggravated by allergies, emotional upset, low immunity, toxin build-up in the body, and brain damage.

Daily treatment can promote calm and encourage mental relaxation. Use only light pressure if treating children.

Follow the treatment plan for sleep disturbance, but use firm pressure on the endocrine areas, to balance the hormones rather than promote sleep.

Visualization

Imagine floating on the surface of a mountain lake. Feel the deep blue water cooling and calming you. Allow your body to dissolve over the surface of the lake. Stay with the calm, relaxing, floating feelings.

Depression and anxiety

Common causes include emotional problems, childbirth, reactions to childhood experiences, and responses to pain or stress that get out of control. Anxiety has similar symptoms to depression, along with an element of fearfulness.

Regular head massage with meditation or visualization calms the mind and promotes a positive self-image.

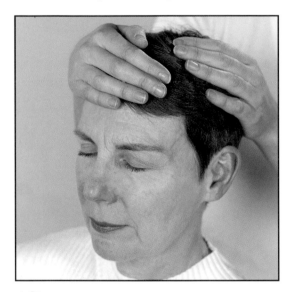

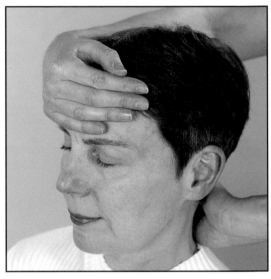

▲ Step one
Relax the scalp using slow, gentle stroking, combing, and light hair pulling all over the head, over and over again. This will take your partner to a deep level of relaxation where her mind and body can let go. Here she needs support rather than stimulation: understanding love and a safe environment in which to release.

Caution
Do not use firm pressure on the top of the head on the very young, the elderly, or anyone suffering from epilepsy, bone disease, or clinical depression.

▲ Step two
Once your partner is deeply relaxed, hold the head with one hand on the back of the neck and the other on the forehead and guide her through the visualization on the opposite page.

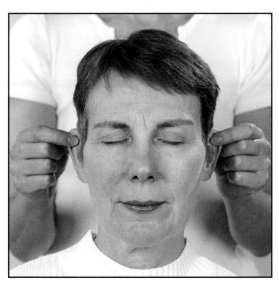

▲ Step 3
Without coming back to the room from the visualization (see right), move on to massaging the shenmen point in the ear (see page 106) for about five minutes as you talk your partner through the candle meditation on page 34. It is the most important point for calming the mind. Pinch firmly with your thumb behind the ear and finger inside, and massage with light rotations.

Visualization

Feel around you a warm, golden glow. Smell the scent of lavender. As you become more aware of the warmth, light, and scents around you, the glow becomes infused with a soft violet light. Allow this light to move slowly into your being. Feel the light reaching through to your heart. Stay with this light. Feel its healing and protection.

Mental exhaustion

Tension can lead to a continuous tensing of the muscles in the neck, upper back, shoulders, and head. This in turn can cause headaches, backache, tight scalp (preventing circulation of blood and nutrients to the hair), tiredness, mental fatigue, and mind and body burnout. The immune system becomes suppressed, leaving the body open to attack from physical, mental, and emotional problems.

Weekly head massage relieves stress, encourages sleep and eating patterns to stabilize, and gives you more energy to cope with stressful situations.

Meditation

Imagine floating in a warm, comforting pink and gold cloud.

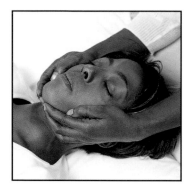 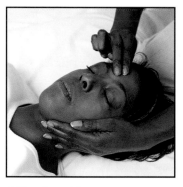 

▲ Treatment one

To balance and strengthen the immune system, massage each of the lymphatic areas (see page 107) for 10–30 seconds. First work up the front of the throat with four finger rotations in horizontal lines. Then use four fingers under the jaw, spreading the fingers to cover the length of the jawbone. Now use four finger rotations behind the ears and around to the base of the skull, followed by light finger kneading and four finger pressure.

Caution

Do not massage these areas on anyone who has cancer.

▲ Treatment two

To stimulate and balance the endocrine system, massage the temples and middle of the forehead with two finger rotations for 10 seconds followed by firm pressure for 10 seconds. Then massage the thyroid area at the base of the throat (see page 107) with two finger rotations for 10 seconds.

▲ Treatment three

As an instant energy booster, pinch the kidney and pancreas points on the ear (see page 106) between thumb and index fingernails and massage for 10–30 seconds. To find these points, put your index finger in the ear, with the edge of the finger nail aligned with the ear hole. Slide it up until it meets the inner ridge and then rock the finger back: the pad of the finger will now be on the kidney and pancreas points. Massage on these points may be painful, but it gives a powerful energy lift.

Chronic fatigue syndrome

Symptoms of this debilitating condition, also known as myalgic encephalomyelitis (ME), include lack of energy, depression, muscular pains, headaches, nausea, and memory loss. Among the suspected causes are viral infection, immune imbalance, psychological or neurological problems, and overuse of antibiotics.

Regular head massage improves feelings of wellbeing, reduces stress, helps to counteract feelings of fatigue and depression, and boosts the immune system.

As someone suffering from this condition may not want to be bothered with massage, you may want to begin with gentle stroking and combing combined with a light meditation, and gradually work up to a full head massage, introducing new techniques each time.

Heart and circulatory conditions

These are aggravated by high blood pressure, excess weight, stress, emotional problems, and imbalances in energy, immunity, and the hormones. In particular, high blood pressure adversely affects the heart muscles, and conditions such as angina and palpitations, as well as accelerating the narrowing of the arteries.

Regular head massage, following the complete plan in chapter five, helps to reduce blood pressure and lower stress levels. It deeply relaxes the muscles, reducing blood vessel constriction and improving the circulation.

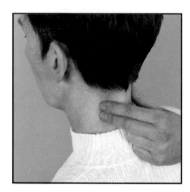

▲ Treatment one

If your partner is sitting down, support the forehead firmly with one hand. With the thumb and fingers of your other hand either side of the spine, rotate strongly up the neck toward the head. When you reach the top of the neck, push with slowly increasing pressure in an upward direction in the hollow just under the base of the skull. At the same time resist the push with your supporting hand. Hold for 20 seconds. You may find your partner's breathing deepens.

Repeat the whole movement twice more, widening your grip on the neck by one fingerwidth each time. This will cover three still points on either side of the spine (see page 105). Finish with a gently rotating massage over the back of the neck.

Treatment two

If your partner is lying down, work rotations with four fingers either side of the neck, with the little fingers next to the spine and the others in a line parallel to the shoulders. This enables the whole neck to be treated in one go. When you reach the base of the skull, hook your fingers under the bony ridge and pull toward you with slowly increasing pressure. A gentle shaking movement at this point encourages the whole body to release tension.

Visualization

See a soft pink light all around your heart. As you relax, feel this light moving through your arteries, veins, and capillaries, healing and strengthening them. Hold this image for as long as you can before allowing it to be absorbed slowly by the rest of your body.

Caution

Do not massage the lymphatic areas on the sides of the face, the throat, across the chin, or behind the ears (see page 107), on anyone who has cancer.

Excess weight

Underlying causes of excess weight can include stress, emotional problems, eating disorders, low self-image, and negative childhood experiences.

Used regularly, this treatment improves self-image, reduces stress, and combats cravings. The visualization can be used during the massage, or whenever food cravings occur.

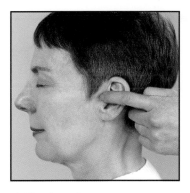

▲ Treatment one
To reduce cravings rotate firmly with a fingertip or nail on the hunger point, in the hollow immediately in front of the ear (see page 106). This is a quick and easy treatment which can be used whenever cravings occur.
Also, to calm the mind, massage the shenmen point in the ear (see page 106). Pinch firmly with your thumb behind the ear and finger inside and massage with light rotations.

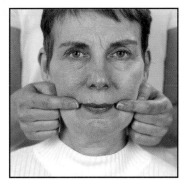

▲ Treatment two
Massaging the lung points at the corners of the mouth (see page 106) with finger rotations or pressure, will help to move negative emotional patterns and improve self-image.

Treatment three
To clear toxins, use the detox massage treatment plan on pages 110–111.

Visualization

See before you a delicious, fattening food. Feel yourself becoming heavy just by looking at it. Now see the food shrinking. As it becomes smaller and smaller you feel lighter and lighter. See it now as small as a pea in your hand. You feel light and free. You no longer see this food as interesting. Let it go.

Digestive problems

Irritable bowel syndrome, stress-related diarrhea, indigestion, constipation, flatulence, and peptic ulcers can all be aggravated by stress, depression, anxiety, negative emotions, and hormone imbalance.

Regular head massage relaxes mind and body, reduces stress, and restores hormone balance, therefore allowing the digestive system to relax, and harmonizing its function.

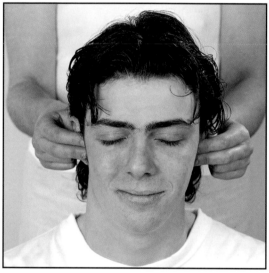

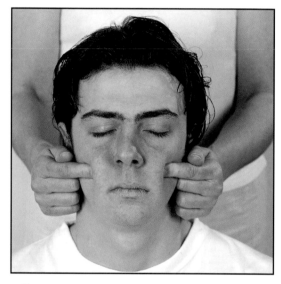

▲ **Step one**
Massage with two finger rotations, pressure, tapping, and stroking at two fingerwidth intervals along the gall bladder channel (see page 105).

▲ **Step two**
Then use finger pressure for 10–30 seconds on the pressure areas for the liver (in the middle of the cheek, pictured above), the kidney points, and the pancreas points (see page 106).

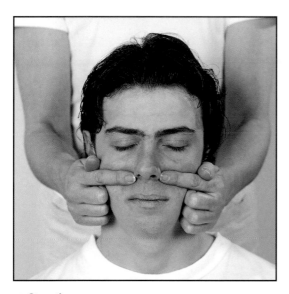

▲ Step three
Press with the length of your fingers along the cheekbones for 10–30 seconds to treat the large intestine area. Then use finger pressure for 10–30 seconds on the bowel point (see page 106).

Step four
To clear toxins, use the detox massage treatment plan on pages 110–111.

Visualization
Imagine you are inside a cool, deep turquoise block of ice. Feel the coolness calming your body through to the center. As your body relaxes, feel the ice melting. Feel bubbles releasing from the ice as it melts. (At this point, if you feel you need to release trapped wind, do so.) As the ice melts it changes to a glowing golden light all around and through you, healing, calming, and regenerating you.

PMS and menstrual problems

Almost 200 symptoms are related to PMS and menstruation. Among the most common are headaches and migraine, low energy, digestive and skin problems, cravings, disturbed sleep, poor concentration, depression, and mood swings.

Regular head massage can rebalance hormones, reduce stress and toxin levels, and boost energy.

During menstruation, concentrate on the orange and the blue in the meditation below, feeling the healing power of the colors moving through you.

Treatment

To balance hormone levels, work on the endocrine areas – the base of the throat, temples, and middle of the forehead – with stroking, rotations, pressure, and tapping. Spend more time within the red of the rainbow meditation (below). This will help to boost your energy and calm mood swings, while supporting and healing your whole being.

Meditation

Imagine you are floating around in a rainbow, feeling the vibration of each color as you move through it. From yellow into orange lifts your mood. From orange to red energizes you and shifts tiredness. The strong healing color purple strengthens you. From the purple change to blue, calming and soothing. Float through to turquoise. You may feel a release within you. Now to green – a healing, calming, and renewing color. The green lightens and becomes a golden yellow. You feel refreshed and regenerated.

Pregnancy

Common pregnancy problems such as nausea, high blood pressure, heartburn, tiredness, and back pain can be eased by head massage. Treatments help balance hormones, boost immune and digestive systems, and calm body and mind.

In the first three months of pregnancy use only stroking, combing, and other light techniques. Later you can use stronger techniques on the back, but the massage should still be lighter than usual.

Use the rainbow meditation on the previous page, spending extra time within the green to help calm the mind.

Caution

In pregnancy do not massage on:
- *the spleen points (see page 105)*
- *the spleen extension channel (see page 105)*
- *the gall bladder area (see page 105)*
- *the midpoint of the shoulders (a point on the gall bladder channel)*

Baby massage

Gentle massage is soothing and relaxing for parent and child, encouraging a strong bond between them. A traditional part of childcare in many cultures, massage stimulates healthy development and has been shown to promote growth in premature babies.

Treatment
Lie your baby across your lap, face down, and stroke with your fingers down the back of the head and along the back. Then, with your baby sitting against your chest, rest your fingers on the baby's shoulders and use your thumbs to stroke gently down over the side of the head. Stroke lightly over the top of the head with your fingers. Keep your movements light and flowing.

Skin conditions

Your skin, more than anything else, reflects your inner being. Conditions such as eczema, dermatitis, psoriasis, acne, and non-infectious skin rashes can all be improved by reducing stress, detoxing the body, and boosting the immune and endocrine systems.

Regular head massage, particularly with strong work across the back, shoulders, neck, and scalp, deeply relaxes the body, enabling its self-healing systems to rejuvenate and repair the skin.

Caution
Do not massage on broken skin or infectious skin rashes.
On sore areas stroke lightly, or hold your hands 1–2in (2–3cm) over the area, focusing healing energy on to it.

Meditation

Imagine yourself surrounded by an aura – an energy cloud of pale yellows, blues, greens, and pinks.

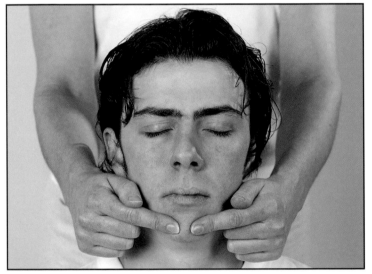

▲ Treatment one
Massaging the pancreas points on either side of the middle of the chin (see page 106) for 10–30 seconds helps to balance blood sugar levels.

Treatment two
To boost immunity, enabling the skin to defend itself more easily, massage the throat, sides of the face, in front of and behind the ears, and down the back of the neck with stroking, four finger rotations, pressure, and tapping.

Caution
Do not massage these areas on anyone who has cancer.

Treatment three
To balance the hormones and calm the mind, use one or two finger pressure, rotations, stroking, and tapping on the endocrine areas – the temples, middle of the forehead, and base of the throat (see page 107).

Treatment four
To clear toxins, use the detox massage treatment plan on pages 110–111.

Mouth and throat problems

Inhaled pollutants, allergens, bacteria, and viruses all enter the body through the nose, mouth, and throat. If you have a tendency to suffer from mouth and throat problems, such as cold sores, oral thrush, toothache, tonsillitis, and laryngitis, this can be aggravated by stress and low immunity.

Use these treatments regularly after a full head massage as a preventive measure, and also to speed recovery from sore throats and other mouth problems.

▲ Treatment one
To stimulate cellular repair in the throat area, massage on the throat point (see page 106). With your finger inside the ear and thumb outside, use pressure and rotations on the underside of the tragus (the gristly flap in front of the ear) for 10–30 seconds.

Treatment two
Calm the mind by massaging the shenmen point in the ear (see page 106). This is on the edge of the dimple just below the outer ridge at the top of the ear, at this dimple's furthest point from the head. Pinch firmly with your thumb behind the ear and finger inside and massage for 10–30 seconds.

▲ Treatment three
To relieve muscular tension and pain in the mouth and throat, pinch the mouth area on the earlobe (see page 106) and rub it between finger and thumb for 10–30 seconds.

Treatment four
The body is less able to cope with pollutants and other toxins if it is already suffering from toxin overload. To clear toxins, use the detox massage treatment plan on pages 110–111.

Visualization
Visualize cool blue water all around you. Feel yourself floating within a sea of healing energy. As you relax, the water becomes a deeper and deeper blue. Stay with the cooling, healing energy of this water.

Respiratory problems

There are many causes of respiratory problems, including viral and bacterial infections, allergies, smoking, irritants such as dust, emotional upset, and hormone changes.

Regular head massage can help to reduce the intensity of attacks in conditions such as emphysema, bronchitis, asthma, catarrh, hay fever, and sinus problems. By relaxing mind and body it gives the self-healing systems a chance to work, and also boosts energy, strengthens the immune system to fight infection, and rebalances the hormones.

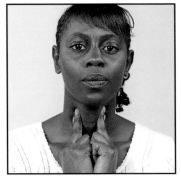

Caution
Do not massage these areas on anyone who has cancer.

▲ Treatment one
To strengthen the lungs, massage the lung pressure points on the outer corners of the mouth (see page 106). Use your index finger to make rotations with firm pressure for about 30 seconds.

▲ Treatment two
An extension to the lung channel runs up the throat, two fingerwidths either side of the windpipe (see page 105). Use rotations with light pressure to massage up both sides of the windpipe simultaneously, treating each point for 30 seconds before moving two fingerwidths up to the next.

Treatment three
To boost the immune system, massage the sides of the face, under the jaw, behind the ears, in the hollow at the back of the neck, up the throat, and over the chin. Use stroking, gentle four finger rotations, and light pressure, all pressing in an upward direction over this whole area.

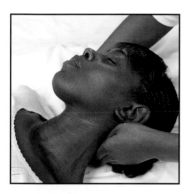

▲ Treatment four

To help relieve the congestion, stiffness, and feverishness that accompanies a cold, massage up the back of the neck on either side of the spine. Use rotations and pressure, working outward in horizontal lines from the middle. If your partner is lying down, place your hands under her neck and use pulsing and stretching.

Treatment five

Strongly massaging up the neck and over the upper back will help the lungs to cope with an asthma attack. Use thumb rotations either side of the spine up the neck, and heel of hand kneading and thumb rotations to work up the spine in horizontal lines, always working outward from the middle.

Treatment six

The lungs are part of the elimination system (see page 104) and so detoxing will help to clear any toxin overload they have to cope with. Use the detox massage treatment plan on pages 110–111.

Visualization

Visualize holding a bright orange marigold. Feel the joyous power in the color. Feel it brightening and clearing your head and chest. Slowly it turns to a clear yellow, calming, and strengthening. Feel all its power and energy moving through you.

Muscular problems

The body contains two types of muscles: voluntary, which control the movements of the limbs for example, and involuntary, which control the movements of the internal organs. Stress puts the whole muscular system under tension, and prolonged stress is the root of many muscular problems.

Head massage relaxes the muscles. When it is combined with visualization, which convinces your involuntary muscles that you are in a safe environment, your body can let go and move into a state of repair and rejuvenation.

Treatment one
Some hormonal imbalances may cause muscle weakness. Massage the endocrine areas at the base of the throat, temples, and the middle of the forehead (see page 107), using stroking, rotations, pressure, and tapping for 30 seconds in each area.

▶ Treatment two
Strong massage of the back, neck, shoulders, and scalp following the routine in chapters three or five, encourages the body to relax and release tension, and improves the circulation. A strong, vigorous treatment is particularly effective for muscle pains and strains anywhere in the body, for stress-related backache, and for problems such as repetitive strain injury (RSI). You may have to start gently and build up to a strong massage if your partner finds the treatment painful. Use the visualization on the opposite page.

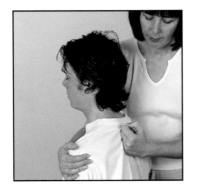

Rheumatism

This is usually taken to mean any disorder that results in pain in the muscles and bones. It can be caused by inflammation of the muscles and is exacerbated by stress, lack of sleep, and emotional upset.

To reduce stress and emotional upset, give regular full head massage following the routines in chapters three or five.

Treatments for sleep problems are on pages 116 and 117.

Arthritis

Arthritic pain arises from inflammation of the tissues in the joints. This inflammation has various causes, including wear and tear on the joint, stress and tension in the muscles, poor circulation, reduced immunity, and a build-up of toxins within the joints and muscles.

Regular head massage reduces stress and tension, rids the muscles of toxins, and improves circulation.

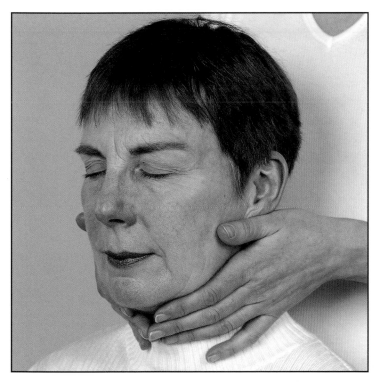

Visualization

Imagine you are sitting in a rose garden in early summer. Close your eyes and be aware of the scents around you. Now gaze at the wonderful colors all around: reds, yellows, oranges, pinks and mauves. Feel their healing energy within your body and mind.

▲ Treatment one

To boost the immune system, stroke lightly up the throat, sides of the face, over the chin, and in front of and behind the ears.

Caution

Do not massage these areas on anyone who has cancer.

Treatment two

To clear toxins, use the detox massage treatment plan on pages 110–111.

Hair and scalp problems

Alopecia or baldness has many causes, including stress, poor circulation, pregnancy, chemotherapy, iron deficiency, and toxin overload. Regular head massage reduces stress, releases toxins, relaxes the scalp, and improves circulation, stimulating the supply of nutrients to the hair roots. Treatment can also prevent dandruff, which can occur when the oils in the scalp are unbalanced and a yeast infection builds up.

The massage should be vigorous and stimulating. There is no visualization to accompany this treatment, since stronger techniques make concentration difficult.

▲ Step one
To loosen the muscles and release constriction around the hair roots, use strong massage on the upper back, shoulders, and neck. Use thumb rotations with firm pressure either side of the spine, working up from the level of the shoulder blade at two fingerwidth intervals.

Then push the muscles out and away from the spine with heel of hand kneading, working up the back in horizontal lines, two fingerwidths apart. Use your body weight to apply pressure to move the muscles so that they become loose, flexible, and relaxed. Hack all over the upper back to give a stimulating finish.

▲ Step two
Now work on the shoulders. Start with the backs of your forearms close to either side of your partner's neck and lean your weight down strongly. Move to a position four fingerwidths toward the arms and repeat.
Now start close to the neck again and work all over the shoulders with thumb rotations and then pressure. Finish with hacking over the shoulders.

Caution
Do not massage the midpoint of the shoulders of anyone who is pregnant.

▲ Step three
Use the strong, vigorous techniques such as rotations, pressure, kneading, hair pulling, scratching, and hacking to work all over the scalp. For people with little hair, or a very short haircut, use the techniques on page 29.
On the neck, work strongly up either side of the spine, with thumb rotations, pressure, and kneading.

Caution
Do not apply strong pressure directly on the spine.

▲ Step four

To strengthen the hair, stimulate circulation, and loosen the scalp, grasp two handfuls of hair, very close to the scalp on the top of the head, and move the scalp backward and forward about 2cm (1in). Repeat on the sides and back of the head. Some people have very tight scalps so you may have to work up to full strength gradually.

Additional treatments

For a very effective anti-dandruff treatment, crush an aspirin and mix it with your regular shampoo. Use once a week.

If your hair is dry or damaged, oils can help bring back the shine and condition. Work a little coconut oil through the hair at the end of the massage and leave it on for 24 hours before shampooing out. Macassar oil is also effective, and is found in some shampoos.

Tinnitus

Sufferers usually hear a ringing, buzzing, roaring, hissing, or whistling noise in one or both ears, and sometimes there is also hearing loss. Causes include injury to the head or ear, infection, toxin build-up in the body, high blood pressure, or heart problems. Stress and muscular tension in the back, neck, and shoulders can make tinnitus worse.

Regular head massage helps to reduce blood pressure, which can lead to a reduction in noises in the ear.

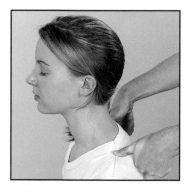

▲ Treatment one
To loosen muscular tension and improve the circulation, use strong massage on the back, shoulders, and neck. Use thumb rotations, leaning in with your body weight to increase the pressure, up either side of the spine on the back and neck, and across the shoulders. Work up the back in horizontal lines using heel of hand kneading from the middle outward. Lean in and push the muscle away from the spine.

Caution
Do not massage the midpoint of the shoulders of anyone who is pregnant. Do not apply strong pressure directly on the spine.

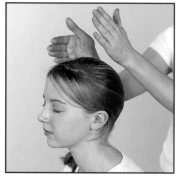

▲ Treatment two
To calm the mind and reduce stress, use hair pulling, pressure, tapping, hacking, and rotations all over the top of the head.

Caution
Do not use firm pressure on the top of the head on the very young, the elderly, or anyone suffering from epilepsy, bone disease, or clinical depression.

Treatment three
To clear toxins, use the detox massage treatment plan on pages 110–111.

Visualization
See a gold light surrounding your head. Feel this light penetrating into the ear. The light drains the noise from the ear, out and away.

Eye strain

Stress and tension in the neck, shoulders, and back of the head affect the muscles in the eyes, so they work less effectively. Therefore before starting to treat the eye area you should thoroughly loosen these areas, following the routine in chapter three. Then use the techniques for the eyes on pages 50 to 51. These tone and condition the muscles in your eyes and, practised daily, can improve your eyesight.

▲ Treatment one

To strengthen the eye muscles, massage round your eye sockets, starting at the bridge of the nose and following a figure of eight. Use very light one finger rotations, working on each point for 2–3 seconds before moving on. Follow your finger with your eyes and complete five circuits before resting your palms over your eyes and relaxing for 5–10 minutes.

Treatment two

Your eyes will become tired if you focus at one distance for some time, for example when reading or looking at a computer screen. To relax them, focus on something in the distance – a view through a window for example – and then move your focus back to something closer, such as the glass in the window. Alternate between the two up to 20 times, holding the focus for one breath in each position.

Epilepsy

Fits or seizures result from a sudden burst of abnormal electrical activity in the brain. Regular head massage, using only a light touch and a lot of stroking and combing in an upward direction, soothes and helps to reduce stress, while meditation promotes calm and relaxation.

Caution

Do not use firm pressure on the top of the head on the very young, the elderly, or anyone suffering from epilepsy, bone disease, or clinical depression.

Visualization

Imagine you are lying in long, green grass. The day is warm and you feel comfortable and relaxed. Allow the green of the grass to permeate your body, bringing a loose, calm feeling to your mind and body.

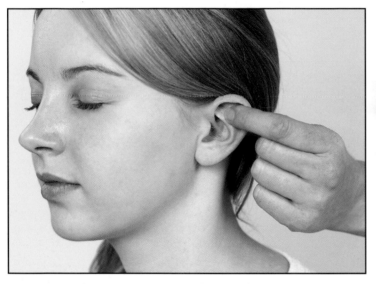

▲ Treatment one
Calm the mind by massaging the shenmen point in the ear (see page 106). Pinch firmly with your thumb behind the ear and finger inside and massage using rotations for 10–30 seconds.

Treatment two
To clear toxins, use the detox massage treatment plan on pages 110–111.

Fainting

For cases of fainting, keep the person lying down to encourage blood flow to the brain and massage the point one fingerwidth above the middle of the upper lip using strong rotations. Remove any false teeth, or the treatment can be painful. The person should soon regain consciousness.

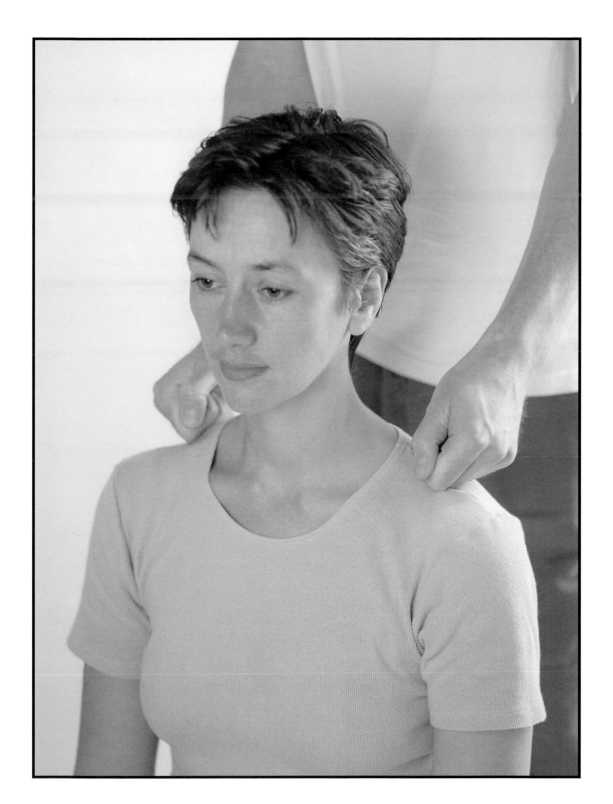

Author's acknowledgements

I would like to express my grateful thanks to all my relatives, friends, students, and teachers who have helped me, in many ways, to complete this book. I would like to thank all at Gaia Books for their hard work and support. I would like to thank fate for its gift of broken bones which, at just the right moment, freed my time for writing.

Publishers' acknowledgements

The publishers would like to thank: Helena Petre and Charlie Ryrie for editorial assistance; Kitty Crossley, and Owen and Jenny Dixon for design assistance; Jackie Beazer, Eilean Bentley, Anne Brabyn, Vicky Eggleton, John Ganly, Sharon Hamilton, Mike Harding, Geoff Hitchings, Adrian Lee, Hazel Morbey, Wilk Morbey, Tom Morbey, Charlotte Morgan and Katherine Pate for modelling; and Lynn Bresler for the index.

Photographic credits

All photography by Steve Teague except: pages 34 and 67 Delilah Dyson; pages 61 and 65 David Woodfall, Woodfall Wild Images; page 63 all Telegraph Colour Library; page 64 Marie O'Hara.

Eilean Bentley

Bibliography

Angelo, Jack
Your Healing Power
1998, Piatkus

Bach, Edward
Heal Thyself
1996, CW Daniel

Brennan, Barbara Ann
Hands of Light
1988, Bantam

Corvo, Joseph
Natural Facelift
1991, Century Random Ltd

Devananda, Swami Vishnu
Meditation and Mantras
1978, OM Lotus Publishing

Honervogt, Tanmaya
Reiki
1998, Gaia Books

Horan, Paula
Empowerment Through Reiki
1990, Lotus Light
Publications

Horan, Paula
Abundance Through Reiki
1995, Lotus Light
Publications

Jarmey, Chris; Mojay, Gabriel
Shiatsu, The Complete Guide
1991, Thorsons

Jarmey, Chris; Tindall, John
*Acupressure for Common
Ailments*
1991, Gaia Books

Lam, Master Kam Chuen
The Way of Energy
1999, Gaia Books

Lundberg, Paul
The Book of Shiatsu
1999, Gaia Books

Shen, Peijian
*Step-by-Step Massage for
Pain Relief*
1996, Gaia Books

*The Hamlyn Encyclopedia
of Complementary Health*
1996, Hamlyn

For information about a CD
of meditations or a video to
accompany this book, please
contact:

Gaia Media
20 High Street
Stroud
Gloucestershire
GL5 1AZ

01453 752985
or:
eileanbentley@lineone.net

For information about
courses in head massage,
reiki, shiatsu, space clearing,
and other therapies, please
contact:

eileanbentley@lineone.net

Index

Massage for Pain Relief

Peijian Shen   ISBN 1 85675 131 7   £11.99
Clear, authoritative text and detailed illustrations demonstrate self-healing techniques as well as how to treat others.

Massage for Common Ailments

Sara Thomas   ISBN 1 85675 031 0   £8.99
This easy-to-use, fully illustrated guide demonstrates how to massage away a variety of common ailments.

Step-by-Step Tui Na

Maria Mercati   ISBN 1 85675 044 2   £11.99
Part of traditional Chinese medicine, Tui Na is a robust, vigorous massage that will improve your health and immunity.

Tui Na Massage for a healthier, brighter child

Maria Mercati   ISBN 1 85675 125 2   £9.99
Massage can treat a number of childhood illnesses including colds, night-crying and teething. It also promotes a healthy immune system and good co-ordination.

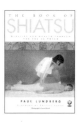

The Book of Shiatsu

Paul Lundberg   ISBN 1 85675 195 3   £12.99
Shiatsu, the Japanese art of touch, restores vitality and health and helps develop your healing powers.

The Tao of Sexual Massage

Stephen Russell and Jurgen Kolb   ISBN 1 85675 001 9   £12.99
Taoist sexual massage energises giver and receiver, improving sex, health and thinking power.

To request a full catalogue of titles published by Gaia Books please call 01453 752985, fax 01453 752987 or write to: Gaia Books Ltd, 20 High Street, Stroud, Gloucestershire GL5 1AZ email: info@gaiabooks.co.uk   website: www.gaiabooks.co.uk